NOISES OFF

A play in three acts

by Michael Frayn

Methuen, Inc.   London/New York

First published in Great Britain in 1982 by Methuen London Ltd., 11 New
Fetter Lane, London EC4P 4EE

Nothing On programme compiled by Michael Frayn, Martin Tickner and
the Company.

Printed in the United States of America

NOISES OFF

AUTHOR'S NOTE

I am even more indebted to other people than usual with this play.
I should particularly like to thank:
Martin Tickner, who commissioned the first short stage prototype,
entitled *Exits*, for a midnight matinee of the Combined Theatrical
Charities, at the Theatre Royal, Drury Lane, on 10 September 1977;
Eric Thompson, who navigated this strange craft, and Denis Quilley,
Patricia Routledge, Edward Fox, Dinsdale Landen, and Polly Adams,
who crewed it;
Michael Codron, who thereupon commissioned the full-length
version, and waited for it with intermittent patience;
Scripts Ltd., of Gerrard St., who typed out the successive editions,
with five different margins and (in Act Two) in two exactly
synchronous columns, without complaint;
Michael Blakemore, whose help with the text went well beyond
what any author could reasonably expect of his director, and whose
ideas are freely incorporated in the following pages.

This is the third edition of the text, and (I hope) the final one. It
incorporates all the modifications that Michael Blakemore and I
introduced when the second and third casts took over in London,
and when the play was produced in New York.

NOISES OFF was first presented, by arrangement with Michael Codron, at the Lyric Theatre Hammersmith on February 23, 1982 and on March 31st by Michael Codron at the Savoy Theatre, London, with the following cast:

DOTTY OTLEY	*Patricia Routledge*
LLOYD DALLAS	*Paul Eddington*
GARRY LEJEUNE	*Nicky Henson*
BROOKE ASHTON	*Rowena Roberts*
POPPY NORTON-TAYLOR	*Yvonne Antrobus*
FREDERICK FELLOWES	*Tony Mathews*
BELINDA BLAIR	*Jan Waters*
TIM ALLGOOD	*Roger Lloyd Pack*
SELSDON MOWBRAY	*Michael Aldridge*

Directed by Michael Blakemore
Designed by Michael Annals
Lighting by Spike Gaden

The first American production of this play was at the Eisenhower Theater in Washington, D.C. on October 22, 1983. NOISES OFF opened at the Brooks Atkinson Theater in New York City on December 11, 1983, with the following cast:

DOTTY OTLEY	*Dorothy Loudon*
LLOYD DALLAS	*Brian Murray*
GARRY LEJEUNE	*Victor Garber*
BROOKE ASHTON	*Deborah Rush*
POPPY NORTON-TAYLOR	*Amy Wright*
FREDERICK FELLOWES	*Paxton Whitehead*
BELINDA BLAIR	*Linda Thorson*
TIM ALLGOOD	*Jim Piddock*
SELSDON MOWBRAY	*Douglas Seale*

Directed by Michael Blakemore
Settings and costumes by Michael Annals
Lighting by Martin Aronstein

ACT ONE

The living room of the Brents' country home. Wednesday
afternoon.
(Grand Theatre, Weston-super-Mare, Monday January 14th)

ACT TWO

The living room of the Brents' country home. Wednesday
afternoon.
(Theatre Royal, Goole, Wednesday matinee, February 13th)

ACT THREE

The living room of the Brents' country home. Wednesday
afternoon.
(Municipal Theatre, Stockton-on-Tees, Saturday April 6th)

The cast of NOISES OFF are performing a play called NOTHING
ON, an extract from the programme of which follows.

Grand Theatre

WESTON-SUPER-MARE

Proprietors: GRAND THEATRE (Weston-super-Mare) LIMITED
General Manager E E A GRADSHAW

The Grand Theatre
Weston-super-Mare
is a Member of the
Grand Group

Commencing Tuesday 15th January for One Week Only

Otstar Productions Ltd

Evenings at 7.45

Matinee: Wednesday
at 2.30

Saturday at 5.00
and 8.30

present

DOTTY OTLEY

BELINDA BLAIR

GARRY LEJEUNE

in

NOTHING ON

by

ROBIN HOUSEMONGER

with

SELSDON MOWBRAY
BROOKE ASHTON
FREDERICK FELLOWES

Directed by **LLOYD DALLAS**

Designed by **GINA STAIRWELL**

Lighting by
CHUCK SPANNER

Costumes by
PATSY BUTTON

WORLD PREMIERE PRIOR TO NATIONAL TOUR!

SMOKING IS NOT PERMITTED IN THE AUDITORIUM

The use of cameras and tape recorders is forbidden

The management reserve the right to refuse admission, also to make
any alteration in the cast which may be rendered necessary by illness
or other unavoidable causes

From the Theatre rules "All exits shall be available for use during all
performances"

"The fire curtain shall be lowered during each performance"

BEHIND
THE DRESSING ROOM DOORS

DOTTY OTLEY makes a welcome return to the stage to create the role of Mrs. Clackett after playing Mrs. Hackett, Britain's most famous lollipop lady ('Ooh, I can't 'ardly 'old me lolly up!') in over 320 episodes of TV's ON THE ZEBRAS. She was born in Malta, the only daughter of Lt. Cdr. Clive Otley, R.N., D.S.M., and trained at the Estelle Birkwood School of Drama and Allied Arts, winning the Bronze Medal, and going on to the Embassy Theatre, Swiss Cottage, where she gained invaluable experience as ASM in successful productions like AS YOU DESIRE and STARCHED APRONS. Understudying Bee Duffell in HADDOCK'S EYES at the New Lindsey Theatre, Notting Hill Gate, and Margaret Lockwood in PETER PAN at the Scala, was followed by The King's Theatre, Peebles for a season, and then the Duke's Players at Lyme Regis for the better part of two seasons, and this in turn led to a prolonged stay in Australia, where she enjoyed some of the biggest successes of her career. When she gets the time she intends writing her memoirs, she says.

BELINDA BLAIR (Flavia Brent) has been on the stage since the age of four, when she made her debut in SINBAD THE SAILOR at the old Croydon Hippodrome as one of Miss Toni Tanner's Ten Tapping Tots. She subsequently danced her way round this country, Southern Africa, and the Far East in shows like ZIPPEDY-DOO-DA! and HERE COMES LES GIRLS! A damaged tendon led to her first straight parts in GOOD TIME GIRL, LADIES OF THE NIGHT, and RING TWICE FOR RITA. More recently she has been seen in such comedy hits as DON'T MR. DUDDLE!, WHO'S BEEN SLEEPING IN MY

BED?, and TWICE TWO IS SEX. She is married to scriptwriter
Terry Wough, who has contributed lead-in material to most of TV's
chat shows. They have two sons and three retrievers.

GARRY LEJEUNE (Roger Tramplemain) was twice winner of the
Rose Bruford Medal for Effort. His many successful tours have
brought him to Weston-super-Mare only once before, when he was
starring in THE ADVENTURES OF A WINDOW DRESSER.
He has made innumerable television appearances, but is perhaps
best-known as 'Cornetto', the ice-cream salesman who stirs the
hearts of all the lollipop ladies in ON THE ZEBRAS. Recently
made his 'big screen' debut in UP THE VIRGIN SOLDIERS, for
which he was nominated as Best Male Newcomer under Forty in
any British Low-Budget Comedy Film by readers of the SUN
newspaper.

SELSDON MOWBRAY (Burglar) first 'trod the boards' in A
MIDSUMMER NIGHT'S DREAM with the Ben Greet Players,
with whom he toured for three years, playing, among other roles,
Moth, Mustardseed, and Nerissa (!) After war service in the Artists'
Rifles, outstanding seasons with various repertory companies across
the length and breadth of Great Britain led to his first West End
play, KELLY'S EYE. Then 'alfresco' in Regent's Park for several
seasons, playing leads. To Stratford thence for Mercutio, King John,
and the Porter in MACBETH. To Hollywood for several good
supporting Roles, including Stand-In to Robert Newton. Back home
he played King Lear in Portsmouth, and joined the BBC Rep for
two months in 1938. Great War No. Two saw him back in Khaki.
Invalided out in 1940 he continued to serve by joining Ensa, and
performing all over the world in many different 'Theatres of War'.
To Dublin in 1946, where he set up his own touring company
playing the Classics, and rivalling the great Agnew Macmaster.
Returned to England in 1952 and set up his own tour—a revival of
MR. CINDERS. Since then, apart from an occasional excursion to
'tread the green', he has been busy writing his autobiography, which
he is thinking of titling HANGING ON THE WALL.

BROOKE ASHTON (Vicki) is probably best known as the girl wearing nothing but 'good, honest, natural froth' in the Hauptbahnhofbrau lager commercial. But she has enjoyed a flourishing stage career, extending from a widely acclaimed Dandini in Hull to six months in the Lebanon with PIXIE PEARLS. Her television appearances range from Girl at Infants' School in ON THE ZEBRAS to Girl in Strip Joint in ON PROBATION. Cinemagoers saw her in THE GIRL IN ROOM 14, where she played the Girl in Room 312.

FREDERICK FELLOWES (Philip Brent) comes from a theatrical family—his parents were a popular specialty dance act of the thirties and forties, 'The Funny Fellowes'. He taught at a prep school near Hayward's Heath before bowing to family tradition and joining the Osmosis Players. There followed successful seasons in Nairobi, Ventnor, and Southwold, and he was most recently seen in the controversial all-male version of THE TROJAN WOMEN. He is happily married, and lives near Crawley, where his wife breeds pedigree dogs. 'If she ever leaves me,' he says, 'it will probably be for an Irish wolfhound!'

ROBIN HOUSEMONGER (Author) was born in Worcester Park, Surrey, into a family 'unremarkable in every way except for an aunt with red hair who used to sing all the high twiddly bits from THE MERRY WIDOW over the tea-table.' He claims to have been the world's most unsuccessful gents hosiery wholesaler, and began writing 'to fill the long hours between one hosiery order and the next.' He turned this experience into his very first play, SOCKS BEFORE MARRIAGE, which ran in the West End for nine years. Several subsequent plays have been produced, and at least one of them broke box office records in Perth, Western Australia. NOTHING ON is his seventeenth play.

LLOYD DALLAS (Director) 'read English at Cambridge, and stagecraft at the Salisbury.' A Commonwealth Scholarship took him to Princeton, where he spent his time 'commuting to New York to see Miller and musicals on Broadway, and Lee Strasberg and Tallulah Bankhead at a party on East 10th St.' Since then Lloyd has directed plays 'in most parts of Britain,' winning the South of Scotland Critics' Circle Special Award in 1968. In 1972 he directed a highly successful season for the National Theatre of Sri Lanka. In recent years Lloyd has probably become best-known for his brilliant series of 'Shakespeare in Summer' productions in the parks of the inner London boroughs.

TIM ALLGOOD (Company Stage Manager) trained for a career in Market Research, and became interested in the theatre only through a chance holiday visit to a local production of THERE'S A GIRL IN MY SOUP. He had got himself taken on by the company as Assistant Stage Manager before he realised that the girl in question was not only in the soup, but also married, with two growing children! During a production of HAMLET at the Lyceum, Portsmouth, he took over the part of Polonius at short notice, but subsequently found himself more in demand on the technical side. His most recent job was with BETROTHED, a thriller by Sam Brennicle, both on the tour prior to its West End opening in December 1980, and again on the tour which followed the conclusion of its successful West End run in January 1981.

POPPY NORTON-TAYLOR (Assistant Stage Manager) is from a family found more often on the boards of leading companies than on the boards with touring companies. Her father is chairman of European Breweries, but has been 'terribly sweet about it all—so far!' After schools in Cheltenham and Montreux she found life far too full to leave time for work. So this is her first job and she is enjoying the challenge enormously. Her hobbies include riding, ski-ing, tennis, reading good books, and loving anything small and furry.

NOTHING ON

by ROBIN HOUSEMONGER

Cast in order of appearance:

Mrs Clackett	**DOTTY OTLEY**
Roger Tramplemain	**GARRY LEJEUNE**
Vicki	**BROOKE ASHTON**
Philip Brent	**FREDERICK FELLOWES**
Flavia Brent	**BELINDA BLAIR**
Burglar	**SELSDON MOWBRAY**
Sheikh	**FREDERICK FELLOWES**

The action takes place in the living-room of the Brents' country home,
on a Wednesday afternoon

for OTSTAR PRODUCTIONS LTD

Company and Stage Manager	**TIM ALLGOOD**
Assistant Stage Manager	**POPPY NORTON-TAYLOR**

Production credits
Sardines by Sardine Services Miss Ashton's lenses by Double Vision Optical Ltd Antique silverware and cardboard boxes by Mrs J. G. H. Norton-Taylor Stethoscope and hospital trolley by Severn Surgical Supplies Straitjacket by Kumfy Restraints Ltd Coffins by G Ashforth and Sons.

We gratefully acknowledge the generous support of EUROPEAN BREWERIES in sponsoring this production

Act One

I

ACT ONE

*The living-room of the Brents' country home. Wednesday
afternoon. (Grand Theatre, Weston-super-Mare, Monday
January 14.)*

   *A delightful 16th-century posset mill, 25 miles from London.
Lovingly converted, old-world atmosphere, many period features.
Fully equipped with every aid to modern living, and beautifully
furnished throughout by owner now resident abroad. Ideal for
overseas company seeking perfect English setting to house senior
executive. Minimum three months let. Apply sole agents: Squire,
Squire, Hackham and Dudley.*

   *THE ACCOMMODATION COMPRISES: an open-plan
living area, with a staircase leading to a gallery. A notable
feature is the extensive range of entrances and exits provided.
On the ground floor the front door gives access to the mature
garden and delightful village beyond. Another door leads to the
elegant panelled study, and a third to the light and airy modern
service quarters. A fourth door opens into a luxurious
bathroom/WC suite, and a full-length south-facing window
affords extensive views. On the gallery level is the door to the
master bedroom, and another to a small but well-proportioned
linen cupboard. A corridor gives access to all the other rooms in
the upper parts of the house. Another beautifully equipped
bathroom/WC suite opens off the landing halfway up the stairs.*

   *All in all, a superb example of the traditional English
set-builder's craft—a place where the discerning theatre-goer will
feel instantly at home.*

As the curtain rises, the award-winning modern telephone is ringing.

Enter from the service quarters MRS CLACKETT, *a housekeeper of character. She is carrying an imposing plate of sardines.*

MRS CLACKETT. It's no good you going on. I can't open sardines and answer the phone. I've only got one pair of feet. (*Puts the sardines down on the telephone table by the sofa, and picks up the phone.*) Hello . . . Yes, but there's no one here, love . . . No, Mr Brent's not here . . . He lives here, yes, but he don't live here now because he lives in Spain . . . Mr Philip Brent, that's right . . . The one who writes the plays, that's him, only now he writes them in Spain . . . No, she's in Spain, too, they're all in Spain, there's no one here . . . Am I in Spain? No, I'm not in Spain, dear. I look after the house for them, only I go home at one o'clock on Wednesday, so that's where *I* am . . . No, because I've got a nice plate of sardines to put my feet up with, and they've got colour here, and it's the royal what's it called—the royal you know—where's the paper, then . . . ?

She searches in the newspaper.

. . . And if it's to do with letting the house then you'll have to ring the house-agents, because they're the agents for the house . . . Squire, Squire, Hackham and who's the other one . . . ? No, they're not in Spain, they're next to the phone in the study. Squire, Squire, Hackham, and hold on, I'll go and look.

She replaces the receiver.

Or so the stage-direction says in Robin Housemonger's play, Nothing On. *In fact, though, she puts the receiver down beside the phone instead.*

Always the same, isn't it. Soon as you take the weight off your feet, down it all comes on your head.

Exit MRS CLACKETT *into the study, still holding the newspaper.*

Or so the stage-direction says. In fact she moves off holding the plate of sardines instead of the newspaper. As she does so, DOTTY

OTLEY, *the actress who is playing the part of* MRS CLACKETT, *comes out of character to comment on the move.*

DOTTY. And I take the sardines. No, I leave the sardines. No, I *take* the sardines.

The disembodied voice of LLOYD DALLAS, *the director of* Nothing On, *replies from somewhere out in the darkness of the auditorium.*

LLOYD. You leave the sardines, and you put the receiver back.

DOTTY. Oh yes, I put the receiver back.

She puts the receiver back, and moves off again with the sardines.

LLOYD. And you leave the sardines.

DOTTY. And I *leave* the sardines?

LLOYD. You *leave* the sardines.

DOTTY. I put the receiver back and I leave the sardines.

LLOYD. Right.

DOTTY. We've changed that, have we, love?

LLOYD. No, love.

DOTTY. That's what I've always been doing?

LLOYD. I shouldn't say that, Dotty, my precious.

DOTTY. How about the words, love? Am I getting some of them right?

LLOYD. Some of them have a very familiar ring.

DOTTY. Only it's like a fruit machine in there.

LLOYD. I know that, Dotty.

DOTTY. I open my mouth, and I never know if it's going to come out three oranges or two lemons and a banana.

LLOYD. Anyway, it's not midnight yet. We don't open till tomorrow. So you're holding the receiver . . .

DOTTY. I'm holding the receiver . . .

LLOYD. 'Squire, Squire, Hackham, and hold on . . .'

DOTTY *resumes her performance as* MRS CLACKETT.

> MRS CLACKETT. Squire, Squire, Hackham, and hold on, don't go away, I'm putting it down.
>
> *She replaces the receiver.*
>
> Always the same, isn't it. Put your feet up for two minutes, and immediately they come running after you.
>
> *Exit* MRS CLACKETT *into the study, still holding the newspaper.*

Only she isn't holding the newspaper.

> *The sound of a key in the lock.*

LLOYD. Hold it.

> *The front door opens. On the doorstep stands* ROGER, *holding a cardboard box. He is about thirty, and has the well-appointed air of a man who handles high-class real estate.*
>
> ROGER. . . . my housekeeper, yes, but this is her afternoon off.

LLOYD. Hold it, Garry. Dotty!

> *Enter* VICKI *through the front door. She is a desirable property in her early twenties, well-built and beautifully maintained throughout.*
>
> ROGER. So we've got the place entirely to ourselves.

LLOYD. Hold it, Brooke. Dotty!

Enter DOTTY *from the study.*

DOTTY. Come back?

LLOYD. Yes, and go out again with the *newspaper.*

DOTTY. The newspaper? Oh, the newspaper.

LLOYD. You put the receiver back, you leave the sardines, and you go out with the newspaper.

GARRY. Here you are, love.

DOTTY. Sorry, love.

GARRY (*embraces her*). Don't worry, love. It's only the technical.

LLOYD. It's the dress, Garry, honey. It's the dress rehearsal.

GARRY. So when was the technical?

LLOYD. So when's the dress? We open tomorrow!

GARRY. Well, we're all thinking of it as the technical. (*To* DOTTY:) Aren't we, love?

DOTTY. It's all those words, my sweetheart.

GARRY. Don't worry about the words, Dotty, my pet.

DOTTY. Coming up like oranges and lemons.

GARRY. Listen, Dotty, your words are fine, your words are better than the, do you know what I mean? (*To* BROOKE:) Isn't that right?

BROOKE. Sorry?

GARRY (*to* DOTTY). I mean, OK, so he's the, you know. Fine. But, Dotty, love, you've been playing this kind of part for, well, I mean, Jesus, Dotty, you know what I mean.

LLOYD. All right? So Garry and Brooke are off, Dotty's holding the receiver . . .

GARRY. No, but here we are, we're all thinking, my God, we open tomorrow, we've only had a fortnight to rehearse, we don't know where we are, but my God, here we are!

DOTTY. That's right, my sweet. Isn't that right, Lloyd?

LLOYD. Beautifully put, Garry.

GARRY. No, but I mean, we've got to play Weston-super-Mare all the rest of this week, then Yeovil, then God knows where, then God knows where else, and so on for God knows how long, and we're all of us feeling pretty much, you know . . . (*To* BROOKE:) I mean, aren't *you?*

BROOKE. Sorry?

LLOYD. Anyway, you're off, Dotty's holding the receiver . . .

GARRY. Sorry Lloyd. But sometimes you just have to come right out with it. You know?

LLOYD. I know.

GARRY. Thanks, Lloyd.

LLOYD. OK, Garry. So you're off . . .

GARRY. Lloyd, let me just say one thing. Since we've stopped. I've worked with a lot of directors, Lloyd. Some of them were geniuses. Some of them were bastards. But I've never met one who was so totally and absolutely . . . I don't know . . .

LLOYD. Thank you, Garry. I'm very touched. Now will you get off the fucking stage?

Exit GARRY *through the front door.*

And, Brooke . . .

BROOKE. Yes?

LLOYD. Are you in?

BROOKE. In?

LLOYD. Are you there?

BROOKE. What?

LLOYD. You're out. OK. I'll call again. And on we go.

Exit BROOKE *through the front door.*

So there you are, holding the receiver.

DOTTY. So there I am, holding the receiver. I put the receiver back and I leave the sardines.

| MRS CLACKETT. Always the same story, isn't it . . .

LLOYD. And you take the newspaper.

She comes back, and picks up the newspaper and the receiver.

DOTTY. I leave the sardines, I take the newspaper.

| MRS CLACKETT. Always the same story, isn't it. It's a weight off
| your mind, it's a load off your stomach.

DOTTY. And off at last I go.

LLOYD. Leaving the receiver.

She replaces the receiver and goes off into the study. Enter
ROGER *as before, with the cardboard box.*

ROGER. . . . my housekeeper, yes, but this is her afternoon off.

Enter VICKI *as before.*

So we've got the place entirely to ourselves.

ROGER *goes back and brings in a flight bag, and closes the*
front door.

I'll just check.

He opens the door to the service quarters. VICKI *gazes round.*

Hello? Anyone at home?

Closes the door.

No, there's no one here. So what do you think?

VICKI. Great. And this is all yours?

ROGER. Just a little shack in the woods, really. Converted posset
mill. Sixteenth-century.

VICKI. It must have cost a bomb.

ROGER. Well, one has to have somewhere to entertain one's
business associates. Someone coming at four o'clock, in fact.
Arab. Oil. You know.

VICKI. Right. And I've got to get those files to our Basingstoke
office by four.

ROGER. Yes, we'll only just manage to fit it in. I mean, we'll
only just do it. I mean . . .

VICKI. Right, then.

ROGER (*puts down the box and opens the flight bag*). We won't
bother to chill the champagne.

VICKI. All these doors.

ROGER. Oh, only a handful, really. Study. Kitchens, and a
self-contained service flat for the housekeeper.

VICKI. Terrific. And which one's the . . . ?

ROGER. What?

VICKI. You know . . .

ROGER. Oh. Through here.

Opens the downstairs bathroom for her.

VICKI. Fantastic.

Exit VICKI *into the bathroom.*
Enter MRS CLACKETT *from the study, without the newspaper.*

MRS CLACKETT. Now I've lost the sardines . . .

Mutual surprise. ROGER *closes the door to the bathroom, and slips the champagne back into the bag.*

ROGER. I'm sorry. I thought there was no one here.

MRS CLACKETT. I'm not here. I'm off, only it's the royal you know, where they wear those hats, and they're all covered in fruit, and who are you?

ROGER. I'm from the agents.

MRS CLACKETT. From the agents?

ROGER. Squire, Squire, Hackham and Dudley.

MRS CLACKETT. Oh. Which one are you, then? Squire, Squire, Hackham, or Dudley?

ROGER. I'm Tramplemain.

MRS CLACKETT. Walking in here as if you owned the place! I thought you was a burgular.

ROGER. No, I just dropped in to . . . go into a few things. Well, to check some of the measurements, do one or two odd jobs.

The bathroom door opens. ROGER *closes it.*

Oh, and a client. I'm showing a prospective tenant over the house.

VICKI (*off, opening the door*): What's wrong with this door?

ROGER. She's thinking of renting it. Her interest is definitely aroused.

Enter VICKI *from bathroom.*

VICKI. That's not the bedroom.

ROGER. The bedroom? No, that's the downstairs bathroom and WC suite. And this is the housekeeper. Mrs Crockett.

MRS CLACKETT. Clackett, dear, Clackett.

VICKI. Oh. Hi.

ROGER. She's not really here.

MRS CLACKETT. Only it's the colour.

ROGER. It's the royal, you know.

MRS CLACKETT. It's black-and-white at home.

ROGER (*to* MRS CLACKETT): Don't worry about us.

MRS CLACKETT (*picks up the sardines*). I'll have the sound on low.

ROGER. We'll just inspect the house.

MRS CLACKETT. Only now I've lost the newspaper.

Exit MRS CLACKETT *into the study, carrying the sardines.*

Only she leaves them behind.

LLOYD. Sardines!

  | ROGER. I'm sorry about this.

LLOYD. Sardines!

  | VICKI. That's all right. We don't want the television, do we?

LLOYD. Sardines!

Enter DOTTY *from the study.*

DOTTY. I've forgotten the sardines.

GARRY. Lloyd! These bloody sardines! We've got to do something about them. We can't go on like this.

LLOYD. Can't go on like what, Garry?

GARRY. OK, it's all right for you, sitting out there, but we've got to *work* with these sardines, we all feel the same. (*To* BROOKE:) Don't we?

BROOKE. Sorry?

GARRY. The sardines.

BROOKE. What sardines?

GARRY (*to* LLOYD). I mean, we're up here, working our backsides off, and there are four plates of sardines coming on in Act One alone. Do you know what I mean?

LLOYD. Poppy! (*To* GARRY:) You want something instead of the sardines? Is that what you're saying? You want Poppy to mash up some banana?

DOTTY. We don't want four plates of mashed banana.

Enter POPPY, *the assistant stage manager, from the wings.*

LLOYD. Poppy, we're changing the sardines.

GARRY. We're not getting at you, Poppy, love.

DOTTY. We think the sardines are lovely.

GARRY (*to* DOTTY). I'd be perfectly happy with the sardines if you were happy with them, love.

DOTTY. I'm happy with them if you're happy with them, love.

LLOYD. So, Garry, honey, what exactly are you saying?

GARRY. What we're saying, Lloyd, is simply this: here we are busting our guts up here and, *Christ!*

LLOYD. I see. Got that, Poppy?

POPPY. Um. Well.

LLOYD. Right. On we go. From Dotty's exit. And, Poppy . . .

POPPY. Yes?

LLOYD. Don't let this happen again.

POPPY. Oh. No.

Exit POPPY *into the wings.*

GARRY. Sorry, Lloyd. I thought we ought to get that straight.

LLOYD. Of course. As long as Dotty's happy.

DOTTY. Absolutely happy, Lloyd, my love.

LLOYD. Will you do something for me, then, Dotty, my precious?

DOTTY. Anything, Lloyd, my sweet.

LLOYD. Take the sardines off with you.

> *Exit* MRS CLACKETT *into study, carrying the sardines.*

ROGER. I'm sorry about this.

VICKI. That's all right. We don't want the television, do we?

ROGER. Only she's been in the family for generations.

VICKI. Great. Come on, then. (*Starts upstairs.*) I've got to be in Basingstoke by four.

ROGER. Perhaps we should just have a glass of champagne.

VICKI. We'll take it up with us.

ROGER. Yes. Well . . .

VICKI. And don't let my files out of sight.

ROGER. No. Only . . .

VICKI. What?

ROGER. Well . . .

VICKI. Her?

ROGER. She has been in the family for generations.

> *Enter* MRS CLACKETT *from the study, with the newspaper but without the sardines.*

MRS CLACKETT. Sardines . . . Sardines . . . It's not for me to say, of course, dear, only I will just say this: don't think twice about it—take the plunge. You'll really enjoy it here.

VICKI. Oh. Great.

MRS CLACKETT (*to* ROGER): Won't she, love?

ROGER. Yes. Well. Yes!

MRS CLACKETT (*to* VICKI): And we'll enjoy having you. (*To* ROGER:) Won't we, love?

ROGER. Oh. Well.

VICKI. Terrific.

MRS CLACKETT. Sardines, sardines. Can't put your feet up on an empty stomach, can you.

Exit MRS CLACKETT *to service quarters.*

VICKI. You see? She thinks it's great. She's even making us sardines!

ROGER. Well . . .

VICKI. I think she's terrific.

ROGER. Terrific.

VICKI. So which way?

ROGER (*picks up the bags*). All right. Before she comes back with the sardines.

VICKI. Up here?

ROGER. Yes, yes.

VICKI. In here?

ROGER. Yes, yes, yes.

Exeunt ROGER *and* VICKI *into mezzanine bathroom.*

VICKI. It's another bathroom.

They reappear.

ROGER. No, no, no.

VICKI. Always trying to get me into bathrooms.

ROGER. I mean in *here.*

Nods at the next door—the first along the gallery. VICKI *leads the way in.* ROGER *follows.*

VICKI. Oh, black sheets! (*Produces one.*)

ROGER. It's the airing cupboard (*Throws the sheet back.*) This one, this one, this one.

He drops the bag and box and struggles nervously to open the second door along the gallery, the bedroom.

VICKI. Oh, you're in a real state!

ROGER. Come on, then.

VICKI. You can't even get the door open.

Exeunt ROGER and VICKI into the bedroom.

Only they can't, because the bedroom door won't open.

The sound of a key in the lock, and the front door opens. On the doorstep stands PHILIP, carrying a cardboard box. He is in his forties, with a deep suntan, and writes attractive new plays with a charming period atmosphere.

PHILIP. . . . Yes, but then this is Mrs Clackett's afternoon off.

LLOYD. Hold it.

Enter FLAVIA. She is in her thirties, the perfect companion piece to the above.

LLOYD. Hold it.

PHILIP. We've got the place entirely to ourselves.

PHILIP brings in a flight bag and closes the door.

Only the door won't stay closed. A pause, while GARRY struggles to open the door upstairs, and FREDERICK struggles to close the door downstairs.

LLOYD. And God said, Hold it. And they held it. And God saw that it was terrible.

GARRY (*to FREDERICK and BELINDA, the actor and actress playing PHILIP and FLAVIA*). Sorry, loves, the door won't open.

BELINDA. Sorry, love, this door won't close.

LLOYD. And God said, Poppy!

FREDERICK. Sorry, everyone. Am I doing something wrong? You know how stupid I am about doors.

BELINDA. Freddie, my sweet, you're doing it perfectly.

FREDERICK. As long as it's not me that's broken it.

Enter POPPY *from the wings.*

LLOYD. And there was Poppy. And God said, Be fruitful and multiply, and fetch Tim to fix the doors.

Exit POPPY *into the wings.*

BELINDA. Oh, I love technicals!

GARRY. She loves technicals! (*Fondly.*) Isn't she just, I mean, Christ, she loves technicals! Dotty! Where's Dotty?

BELINDA. Everyone's always so nice to everyone.

GARRY. Oh! Isn't she just, I mean, she really is, isn't she.

Enter DOTTY *from the service quarters.*

(*To* DOTTY:) Belinda's being all, you know.

BELINDA (*holding out an arm to* FREDERICK). But Freddie, my precious, don't you like a nice all-night technical?

FREDERICK. The only thing I like about technicals is you get a chance to sit on the furniture.

He sits.

BELINDA. Oh, Freddie, my precious! It's lovely to see you cheering up and making jokes.

She sits beside him, and embraces him.

FREDERICK. Oh, was that a joke?

BELINDA. This is such a lovely company to work with. It's such a happy company.

DOTTY. Wait till we've got to Stockton-on-Tees in twelve weeks' time.

BELINDA (*sits*). Are *you* all right, Lloyd, my precious?

LLOYD. I'm starting to know what God felt like when he sat out there in the darkness creating the world. (*He takes a pill.*)

BELINDA. What did he feel like, Lloyd, my love?

LLOYD. Very pleased he'd taken his Valium.

BELINDA. He had six days, of course. We've only got six hours.

LLOYD. And God said, Where the hell is Tim?

Enter from the wings TIM, *the company stage manager. He is exhausted.*

And there the hell *was* Tim. And God said, Let there be doors, that open when they open, and close when they close.

TIM. Do something?

LLOYD. Doors.

TIM. I was getting the bananas. For the sardines.

LLOYD. Doors.

TIM. Doors?

LLOYD. I bet God had a stage manager who understood English, too.

BELINDA. Tim, my love, this door won't close.

GARRY. And the bedroom won't, you know.

TIM. Oh, right. (*Sets to work on the doors.*)

BELINDA (*to* LLOYD). He hasn't been to bed for forty-eight hours.

LLOYD. Don't worry, Tim. Only another twenty-four hours, and it'll be the end of the day.

LLOYD *comes up on stage.*

BELINDA. Oh, look, he's come down on earth amongst us.

LLOYD. Listen. Since we've stopped anyway. OK, it took two days to get the set up, so we shan't have time for a dress rehearsal. Don't worry. Think of the first night as a dress rehearsal. If we can just get through the play once tonight for doors and sardines. That's what it's all about. Doors and sardines. Getting on—getting off. Getting the sardines on—getting the sardines off. That's farce. That's the theatre. That's life.

BELINDA. Oh God, Lloyd, you're so deep.

LLOYD. So just keep going. Bang, bang, bang. Bang you're on. Bang you've said it. Bang you're off. And everything will be perfectly where's Selsdon?

BELINDA. Oh God.

GARRY. Oh God oh God oh God.

BELINDA. Selsdon!

GARRY. Selsdon!

LLOYD. Poppy!

DOTTY (to LLOYD). I thought he was in front, with you?

LLOYD. I thought he was round the back, with you?

Enter POPPY *from the wings.*

Is Mr Mowbray in his dressing-room?

Exit POPPY *into the wings.*

FREDERICK. Oh, I don't think he would. Not at a technical. (*To* BROOKE:) Would he?

BROOKE. Would who?

GARRY. Selsdon. We can't find him!

FREDERICK. I'm sure he wouldn't. Not at a technical.

DOTTY. Half a chance, he would.

BROOKE. Would what?

GARRY, DOTTY *and* LLOYD *make gestures to her of tipping a glass, or raising the elbow, or screwing the nose.*

BELINDA. Now come on, my sweets, be fair! We don't know.

FREDERICK. Let's not jump to any conclusions.

LLOYD. Let's just get the understudy dressed. Tim!

TIM. Yes?

LLOYD. Hurry up with those doors. You're going on for Selsdon.

TIM. Oh. Right.

DOTTY. He shouldn't have been out of sight! I said, he must never be out of sight!

BELINDA. He's been as good as gold all the way through rehearsals.

GARRY. Yes, because in the rehearsal room it was all, I don't know, but there we were, do you know what I mean?

LLOYD. You mean you could see everyone.

GARRY. And here it's all, you know.

LLOYD. Split into two. There's a front and a back. And instantly we've lost him.

Enter POPPY *from the wings.*

POPPY. He's not in his dressing-room.

DOTTY. You've looked in the lavatories?

POPPY. Yes.

DOTTY. And the scenery dock and the prop room and the paint store?

POPPY. Yes.

FREDERICK (*to* DOTTY). You've worked with him before, of course.

LLOYD (*to* POPPY). Ring the police.

Exit POPPY *into the wings.*

(*To* TIM:) Finished the doors? Right, get the gear on.

Exit TIM *into the wings.*

Enter SELSDON MOWBRAY *from the back of the stalls. He is in his seventies, and is wearing his burglar gear. He comes down the aisle during the following dialogue, and stands in front of the stage, watching everyone on it.*

I'm sorry, Dotty, my love.

DOTTY. No, it's my fault, Lloyd, my love.

LLOYD. I cast him.

DOTTY. 'Let's give him one last chance,' I said. I mean, what can you do? We were in weekly rep together in Peebles.

GARRY (*to* DOTTY): It's my fault, my precious—I shouldn't have let you. This tour isn't just, do you know what I mean? For her, this is her life savings!

LLOYD. We know that, Garry, love.

BELINDA *puts a hand on* DOTTY's *arm.*

DOTTY. I'm not trying to make my fortune.

FREDERICK. Of course you're not, Dotty.

BELINDA. We know that.

DOTTY. I just wanted to put a little something by.

BELINDA. We know, love.

GARRY. Just something to buy a little house that she could I mean Jesus, that's not so much to ask.

BELINDA (*to* BROOKE): Now come on, my sweet. You mustn't blame yourself.

BROOKE. Sorry?

BELINDA. You're not going to cry. I'm not going to let you cry.

BROOKE. No, I've got something behind my lens.

FREDERICK. Yes, it's not Brooke's fault. You couldn't expect her to keep an eye on anyone.

DOTTY (*points at* SELSDON *without seeing him*). But he was standing right there in the stalls before we started! I saw him!

BROOKE. Who are we talking about now?

BELINDA. It's all right, my sweet. We know you can't see anything.

LLOYD *takes one of his tranquilliser pills.*

BROOKE. You mean *Selsdon?* I'm not *blind.* I can see *Selsdon.*

They all turn and see him.

BELINDA. Selsdon!

GARRY. Oh my God, he's here all the time!

LLOYD. Standing there like Hamlet's father.

FREDERICK. My word, Selsdon, you gave us a surprise. We thought you were . . . We thought you were—not there.

DOTTY. Where have you been, Selsdon?

BELINDA. Are you all right, Selsdon?

LLOYD. Speak to us!

SELSDON. Is it a party?

BELINDA. 'Is it a party?'!

SELSDON. Is it? How killing! I got it into my head there was going to be a rehearsal.

He goes up on to the stage.

I was having a little postprandial snooze at the back of the stalls so as to be ready for the rehearsal.

BELINDA. Isn't he lovely?

LLOYD. Much lovelier now we can see him.

SELSDON. So what are we celebrating?

BELINDA. 'What are we celebrating?'!

Enter TIM *from the wings.*

LLOYD. Tim, you look strained and anxious. You're not trying to do too much, are you?

TIM. I can't find the gear. I've looked all through his dressing-room. I've looked all through the wardrobe.

LLOYD *indicates* SELSDON.

Oh.

SELSDON. Beer? In the wardrobe?

LLOYD. No, Selsdon. Tim, you need a break. Why don't you sit down quietly upstairs and do all the company's VAT?

TIM. I'll just do the bananas first.

Exit TIM *into the wings.*

BELINDA. He has been on his feet for forty-eight hours, Lloyd.

LLOYD (*calls*): Don't fall down, Tim. We may not be insured.

SELSDON. So what's next on the bill?

LLOYD. Well, Selsdon, I thought we might try a spot of rehearsal.

SELSDON. Oh, I won't, thank you.

LLOYD. You *won't?*

SELSDON. You all go ahead. I'll sit and watch you. This is the beer in the wardrobe, is it?

BELINDA. No, my sweet, he wants us to rehearse.

SELSDON. Yes, but I think we've got to rehearse, haven't we?

LLOYD. Rehearse, yes! Well done, Selsdon. I knew you'd think of something. Right, from Belinda and Freddie's entrance . . .

Enter POPPY *from the wings, alarmed.*

Oh my God, what's happened now?

POPPY. The police!

LLOYD The *police?*

POPPY. They've found an old man. He was lying unconscious in a doorway just across the street.

LLOYD. Oh. Yes. Thank you.

POPPY. They say he's very dirty and rather smelly, and I thought, oh my God, because—

LLOYD. Thank you, Poppy.

POPPY. Because when you get close to Selsdon—

BELINDA. Poppy!

POPPY. No, I mean, if you stand anywhere near Selsdon you can't help noticing this very distinctive . . .

She stops, sniffing.

SELSDON (*to* POPPY, *putting an arm round her*): I'll tell you something, Poppy. Once you've got it in your nostrils you never forget it. Sixty years now, and the smell of the theatre still haunts me.

Exit SELSDON *into the study.*

BELINDA. Oh, bless him!

LLOYD. Tell me, Poppy, love—how did you get a job like this, that requires tact and understanding? You're not somebody's girl-friend, are you?

POPPY *gives him a startled look.*

BELINDA. Don't worry, Poppy, my sweet. He truly did not hear.

Enter SELSDON *from the study.*

SELSDON. *Not* here?

LLOYD. Yes, yes,—there!

BELINDA. Sit down, my precious.

DOTTY. Go back to sleep.

LLOYD. You're not on for another twenty pages yet.

SELSDON. I think I might go back to sleep. I'm not on for another twenty pages yet.

Exit SELSDON *into the study. Exit* POPPY *into the wings.*

LLOYD. And on we go.

He goes back down into the auditorium.

Dotty in the kitchen, wildly roasting sardines. Freddie and Belinda waiting impatiently outside the front door. Garry and Brooke disappearing tremulously into the bedroom. Time sliding irrevocably into the past.

Exeunt DOTTY *into the service quarters,* GARRY *and* BROOKE *upstairs into the bedroom, and* FREDERICK *through the front door.*

BELINDA (*to* LLOYD, *with lowered voice*): Aren't they sweet?

LLOYD. What?

BELINDA. Garry and Dotty.

LLOYD. Garry and Dotty?

BELINDA. Sh!

LLOYD (*lowers his voice*): What? You mean they're . . . ?

BELINDA. It's supposed to be a secret.

LLOYD. But she's old enough to be—

BELINDA. Sh!

LLOYD. *Garry?* And *Dotty?* Tramplemain and Mrs Clackett?

BELINDA. Didn't you know?

LLOYD (*in his ordinary voice*): I'm just God, Belinda, love. I'm just the one with the English degree, I don't know anything.

Enter GARRY *from the bedroom.*

GARRY. What's happening?

LLOYD. You tell me, Garry, honey.

Exit BELINDA *through the front door.*

GARRY. I mean, what are we waiting for?

Enter DOTTY *from the service quarters, inquiringly.*

LLOYD. I don't know what you're waiting for, Garry. Her sixteenth birthday?

GARRY. What?

LLOYD. Or maybe just the cue. Brooke!

Exit DOTTY *to the service quarters.*
Enter BROOKE *from the bedroom.*

LLOYD. 'You can't even get the door open.'

| VICKI. You can't even get the door open.

LLOYD. Door closed, love.

GARRY *closes the door.*

| VICKI. You can't even get the door open.

Exeunt ROGER *and* VICKI *into the bedroom.*
Enter PHILIP *through the front door.*

PHILIP. Yes, but this is Mrs Clackett's afternoon off.

Enter FLAVIA.

We've got the place entirely to ourselves.

PHILIP *brings in the flight bag and closes the door.*

FLAVIA. Look at it!

PHILIP. Do you like it?

FLAVIA. I can't believe it!

PHILIP. The perfect place for an assignation.

FLAVIA. Home.

PHILIP. Home.

FLAVIA. Our little secret hideaway.

PHILIP. The last place on earth anyone will look for us.

FLAVIA. It's rather funny, creeping in like this.

PHILIP. It's damned serious! If Inland Revenue find out we're
   in the country, even for one night, bang goes our claim to
   be resident abroad—bang goes most of this year's income. I
   feel like an illegal immigrant.

FLAVIA. I'll tell you what I feel like.

PHILIP. Champagne? (*Takes a bottle out of the box.*)

FLAVIA. I wonder if Mrs Clackett's aired the beds.

PHILIP. Darling!

FLAVIA. Well, why not? No children. No friends dropping in.
   We're absolutely on our own.

PHILIP. True. (*Picks up the bag and box and ushers* FLAVIA
   towards the stairs.) There is something to be said for being a
   tax exile.

FLAVIA. Leave those!

He drops the bag and box and kisses her. She flees upstairs, laughing, and he after her.

PHILIP. Sh!

FLAVIA. What?

PHILIP. Inland Revenue may hear us!

They creep to the bedroom door.
Enter MRS CLACKETT *from the service quarters carrying a fresh plate of sardines.*

MRS CLACKETT (*to herself*): What I did with that first lot of sardines I shall never know.

She puts the sardines on the telephone table and sits on the sofa.

PHILIP *and* FLAVIA (*looking down from the gallery*): Mrs Clackett!

MRS CLACKETT *jumps up.*

MRS CLACKETT. Oh, you give me a turn! My heart jumped right out of my boots!

PHILIP. So did mine!

FLAVIA. We thought you'd gone!

MRS CLACKETT. I thought you was in Spain!

PHILIP. We are! We are!

FLAVIA. You haven't seen us!

PHILIP. We're not here!

MRS CLACKETT. Oh, like that, is it? The income tax are after you?

FLAVIA. They would be, if they knew we were here.

MRS CLACKETT. All right, then, love. You're not here. I haven't seen you. Anybody asks for you, I don't know nothing. Off to bed, are you?

PHILIP. Oh . . .

FLAVIA. Well . . .

MRS CLACKETT. That's right. Nowhere like bed when they all get on top of you. You'll want your things, look. (*Indicates the bag and box.*)

PHILIP. Oh. Yes. Thanks.

He comes downstairs, and picks up the bag and box.

MRS CLACKETT (*to* FLAVIA): Oh, and that bed hasn't been aired, love.

FLAVIA. I'll get a hot water bottle.

Exit FLAVIA *into the mezzanine bathroom.*

MRS CLACKETT. I've put all your letters in the study, dear.

PHILIP. Letters? What letters? You forward all the mail, don't you?

MRS CLACKETT. Not the ones from the income tax, dear. I don't want to spoil your holidays.

PHILIP. Oh my God. Where are they?

MRS CLACKETT. I've put them all in the little pigeonhouse.

PHILIP. In the pigeonhouse?

MRS CLACKETT. In the little pigeonhouse in your desk, love.

Exeunt MRS CLACKETT *and* PHILIP *into the study.* PHILIP *is still holding the bag and box.*

Only he remains on, and DOTTY *remains in the doorway waiting for him.*

Enter ROGER *from the bedroom, still dressed, tying his tie.*

ROGER. Yes, but I could hear voices!

Enter VICKI *from the bedroom in her underwear.*

VICKI. Voices? What sort of voices?

LLOYD. Hold it. Freddie, what's the trouble?

FREDERICK. Lloyd, you know how stupid I am about moves. Sorry, Garry—sorry, Brooke—it's just my usual dimness. (*To* LLOYD:)

But why do I take the things off into the study? Wouldn't it be more natural if I left them on?

LLOYD. No.

FREDERICK. I just thought it might be somehow more logical.

LLOYD. No.

FREDERICK. Lloyd, I know it's a bit late in the day to go into all this . . .

LLOYD. No, Freddie, we've got several more minutes left before we open.

Enter BELINDA *from the mezzanine bathroom, to wait patiently.*

FREDERICK. Thank you, Lloyd. As long as we're not too pushed. But I've never understood why he carries an overnight bag and a box of groceries into the study to look at his mail.

GARRY. Because they have to be out of the way for my next scene!

FREDERICK. I see that.

BELINDA. And Freddie, my sweet, Selsdon needs them in the study for *his* scene.

FREDERICK. I see that . . .

LLOYD. Selsdon—where is he? Is he there?

BELINDA (*calls, urgently*): Selsdon!

DOTTY (*likewise*): Selsdon!

GARRY (*likewise*): Selsdon!

Enter SELSDON *through the window in haste.*

SELSDON. Am I on?

OMNES. No, no, no.

SELSDON. I thought I heard my voice.

LLOYD. No, no, no. Back to sleep, Selsdon. Another ten pages yet.

SELSDON. Oh.

Exit SELSDON *through the window.*

FREDERICK. All right, I see all that.

LLOYD (*faintly*): Oh, no!

FREDERICK. I just don't know why I take them.

LLOYD *comes up on stage.*

LLOYD. Freddie, love, why does anyone do anything? Why does that other idiot walk out through the front door holding two plates of sardines? (*To* GARRY:) I mean, I'm not getting at you, love.

GARRY. Of course not, love. (*To* FREDERICK:) I mean, why *do* I? (*To* LLOYD:) I mean, Jesus, when you come to think about it, why *do* I?

LLOYD. Who knows?

GARRY. Who knows, you see, Freddie, love?

LLOYD (*to* FREDERICK): The wellsprings of human action are deep and cloudy. Maybe something happened to you as a very small child which made you frightened to let go of groceries.

BELINDA. Or it could be genetic.

GARRY. Yes, or it could be, you know.

LLOYD. It could well be.

FREDERICK. Of course. Thank you. I understand all that. But . . .

LLOYD. Freddie, love, I'm telling you—I don't know. I don't think the author knows. I don't know why the author came into this industry in the first place. I don't know why any of us came into it.

FREDERICK. All the same, if you could just give me a reason I could keep in my mind . . .

LLOYD. All right, I'll give you a reason. You carry those groceries into the study, Freddie, honey, because it's just slightly after midnight, and we're not going to be finished before we open tomorrow night. Correction—before we open *tonight.*

FREDERICK *nods, and exits into the study.* DOTTY *silently follows him.* GARRY *and* BROOKE *go silently back into the bedroom.* LLOYD *returns to the stalls.*

And on we go. From after Freddie's exit, *with* the groceries.

BELINDA (*keeping her voice down*): Lloyd, sweetheart, his wife left him this morning.

LLOYD. Oh. Freddie!

Enter FREDERICK *from the study.*

I think the point is that you've had a great fright when she mentions income tax, and you feel very insecure and exposed, and you want something familiar to hold on to.

FREDERICK (*with humble gratitude*): Thank you, Lloyd.

Exit FREDERICK *into the study.*

BELINDA (*to* LLOYD): Bless you, my sweet.

LLOYD. And on we merrily go.

Exit BELINDA *into the mezzanine bathroom.*

'Yes, but I could hear voices . . .'

Enter ROGER *from the bedroom, still dressed, tying his tie.*

ROGER. Yes, but I could hear voices!

Enter VICKI *from the bedroom in her underwear.*

VICKI. Voices? What sort of voices?

ROGER. People's voices.

VICKI. But there's no one here.

ROGER. Darling, I saw the door-handle move! It could be someone from the office, checking up.

VICKI. I still don't see why you've got to put your tie on to look.

ROGER. Mrs Clockett.

VICKI. Mrs Clockett?

ROGER. She's been in the family for generations.

VICKI (*looks over the bannisters*): Oh, look, she's opened our sardines.

She moves to go downstairs. ROGER *grabs her.*

ROGER. Come back!

VICKI. What?

ROGER. I'll fetch them! You can't go downstairs like that.

VICKI. Why not?

ROGER. Mrs Crackett.

VICKI. Mrs Crackett?

ROGER. She's irreplaceable.

Enter MRS CLACKETT *from the study. She is carrying the first plate of sardines.*

MRS CLACKETT (*to herself*): Sardines here. Sardines there. It's like a Sunday school outing.

ROGER *pushes* VICKI *through the first available door, which happens to be the linen cupboard.*

Oh, you're still poking around, are you?

ROGER. Yes, still poking—well, still around.

MRS CLACKETT. In the airing cupboard, were you?

ROGER. No, no. (*The linen cupboard door begins to open. He slams it shut.*) Well, just checking the sheets and pillow-cases. Going through the inventory.

He starts downstairs.

Mrs Blackett . . .

MRS CLACKETT. Clackett, dear, Clackett.

She puts down the sardines beside the other sardines.

ROGER. Mrs Clackett. Is there anyone else in the house, Mrs Clackett?

MRS CLACKETT. I haven't seen no one, dear.

ROGER. I thought I heard voices.

MRS CLACKETT. Voices? There's no voices here, love.

ROGER. I must have imagined it.

PHILIP (*off*): Oh my God!

   ROGER, *with his back to her, picks up both plates of sardines.*

ROGER. I beg your pardon?

MRS CLACKETT (*mimics* PHILIP): Oh my God!

ROGER. Why, what is it?

MRS CLACKETT. Oh my God, the study door's open.

She crosses and closes it. ROGER *looks out of the window.*

ROGER. There's another car outside! That's not Mr Hackham's, is it? Or Mr Dudley's?

Exit ROGER *through the front door, holding both plates of sardines. Enter* FLAVIA *from the mezzanine bathroom, carrying a hot water bottle. She sees the linen cupboard door swinging open as she passes, pushes it shut, and turns the key.*

FLAVIA. Nothing but flapping doors in this house.

Exit FLAVIA *into the bedroom.*
Enter from the study PHILIP, *holding a tax demand and its envelope.*

PHILIP. '. . . final notice . . . steps will be taken . . . distraint . . . proceedings in court . . .'

MRS CLACKETT. Oh yes, and that reminds me, a gentleman come about the house.

PHILIP. Don't tell me. I'm not here.

MRS CLACKETT. He says he's got a lady quite aroused.

PHILIP. Leave everything to Squire, Squire, Hackham and Dudley.

MRS CLACKETT. All right, love. I'll let them go all over, shall I?

PHILIP. Let them do anything. Just so long as you don't tell anyone we're here.

MRS CLACKETT. So I'll just sit down and turn on the . . . sardines, I've forgotten the sardines! I don't know—if it wasn't fixed to my shoulders I'd forget what day it was.

Exit MRS CLACKETT *to the service quarters.*

PHILIP. I didn't get this! I'm not here. I'm in Spain. But if I didn't get it I didn't open it.

Enter FLAVIA *from the bedroom. She is holding the dress that* VICKI *arrived in.*

FLAVIA. Darling, I never had a dress like this, did I?

PHILIP (*abstracted*): Didn't you?

FLAVIA. I shouldn't buy anything as tarty as this . . . Oh, it's not something you gave me, is it?

PHILIP. I should never have touched it.

FLAVIA. No, it's lovely.

PHILIP. Stick it down. Put it back. Never saw it.

Exit PHILIP *into study.*

FLAVIA. Well, I'll put it in the attic, with all the other things you gave me that are too precious to wear.

Exit FLAVIA *along the upstairs corridor.*
Enter ROGER *through the front door, still carrying both plates of sardines.*

ROGER. All right, all right . . . Now the study door's open again! What's going on?

He puts the sardines down—one plate on the telephone table, where it was before, one near the front door—and goes towards the study, but stops at the sound of urgent knocking overhead. (*Knocking*)

Knocking! (*Knocking*) Upstairs!

Runs upstairs. Knocking.

Oh my God, there's something in the airing cupboard!

Unlocks it and opens it. Enter VICKI.

Oh, it's you.

VICKI. Of course it's me! You put me in here! In the dark! With all black sheets and things!

ROGER. But, darling, why did you lock the door?

VICKI. Why did *I* lock the door? Why did *you* lock the door!

ROGER. *I* didn't lock the door!

VICKI. *Someone* locked the door!

ROGER. Anyway, we can't stand here like this.

VICKI. Like what?

ROGER. In your underwear.

VICKI. OK, I'll take it off.

ROGER. In here, in here!

Ushers her into the bedroom.

Only she remains on, blinking anxiously, and peering about the floor. GARRY *waits for her, holding the bedroom door open.*

Enter PHILIP *from the study, holding the tax demand, the envelope, and a tube of glue.*

PHILIP. Darling, this glue. It's not that special quick-drying sort, is it, that you can never get unstuck . . . ?

LLOYD. Hold it.

| PHILIP. Oh, Mrs Clackett's made us some sardines.

LLOYD. Hold it. We have a problem.

FREDERICK (*to* BROOKE): Oh, bad luck! Which one is it this time?

BROOKE. Left.

GARRY (*calls to people off*): It's the left one, everybody!

OMNES (*off*). Left one!

Enter DOTTY, BELINDA, *and* POPPY.

FREDERICK. It could be anywhere.

GARRY (*looks over the edge of the gallery*): It could have gone over the thing and fallen down, you know—and then bounced somewhere else again.

BROOKE *comes downstairs. They all search hopelessly.*

POPPY. Where did you last see it?

BELINDA. She *didn't* see it, poor sweet! It was in her eye!

GARRY (*comes downstairs*): It was probably on 'Why did *I* lock the door?' She opens her eyes very sort of, you know. Don't you, my sweet? I always feel I ought to rush forward and . . .

He rushes forward, hands held out.

DOTTY. Mind where you put your feet, my love.

FREDERICK. Yes, everyone look under their feet.

GARRY. No one move their feet.

BELINDA. Everyone put their feet back exactly where they were.

FREDERICK. Pick your feet up one by one.

They all trample about, looking under their feet, except BROOKE, *who crouches with her good eye at floor level.* LLOYD *comes up on stage.*

LLOYD. Brooke, love, is this going to happen during a performance? We don't want the audience to miss their last buses and trains.

BELINDA. She'll just carry on. Won't you, my love?

FREDERICK. But can she see anything without them?

LLOYD. Can she hear anything without them?

BROOKE (*suddenly realising that she is being addressed*): Sorry?

She straightens up sharply. Her head comes in abrupt contact with POPPY'*s face.*

POPPY. Ugh!

BROOKE. Oh. Sorry.

BROOKE jumps up to see what damage she has done to POPPY, *and steps backward on to* GARRY'*s hand.*

GARRY. Ugh!

BROOKE. Sorry?

DOTTY hurries to his aid.

DOTTY. Oh my poor darling! (*To* BROOKE:) You stood on his hand!

FREDERICK claps a handkerchief to his nose.

BELINDA. Oh, look at Freddie, the poor love!

FREDERICK (*looks into the handkerchief*): Excuse me.

Exit FREDERICK *hurriedly.*

LLOYD. What's the matter with *him*?

BELINDA. He's just got a little nosebleed, my sweet.

LLOYD. A nosebleed? No one touched him!

BELINDA. No, he's got a thing about violence. It always makes his nose bleed.

LLOYD. But where's he gone?

BELINDA. Well, he's got a thing about blood.

BROOKE. Sorry. Sorry. (*To* LLOYD:) I thought you said something to me.

LLOYD. Yes.

He picks up a vase and hands it to her.

Just go and hit the box-office manager with this, and you'll have finished off live theatre in Weston-super-Mare.

BROOKE. Anyway, I've found it.

BELINDA. She's found it!

DOTTY. Where was it, love?

BROOKE. In my eye.

GARRY. In her eye!

BELINDA (*hugs her*). Well done, my sweet.

LLOYD. Not in your left eye?

BROOKE. It had gone round the side.

BELINDA. I knew it hadn't gone far. Are you all right, Poppy, my sweet?

POPPY. I think so.

LLOYD. All right, clear the stage. Walking wounded carry the stretcher cases.

LLOYD returns to the stalls, DOTTY to the service quarters, POPPY to the wings. BELINDA, GARRY and BROOKE go upstairs. Enter FREDERICK.

BELINDA. Are you all right, Freddie, my pet?

FREDERICK. Fine. It's just that I've got this thing about, well, I won't say the word.

BELINDA. We all understand, my precious.

LLOYD. Right, then. On we bloodily stagger. Oh, sorry, Freddie. Let me rephrase that. On we blindly stumble. Brooke, I withdraw that.

Exit BELINDA along upstairs corridor, FREDERICK into study.

From your exit, anyway. 'OK, I'll take it off.—In here, in here.' Where's Selsdon?

GARRY. Selsdon!

LLOYD. Selsdon!

Enter SELSDON through the front door.

SELSDON. I think she might have dropped it out here somewhere.

LLOYD. Good. Keep looking. Only another five pages, Selsdon.

Exit SELSDON through the front door.

'Anyway, we can't stand here like this.—Like what?—In your underwear.—OK, I'll take it off . . .'

ROGER. In here, in here!

Ushers her into the bedroom.
Enter PHILIP from the study, holding the tax demand, the envelope, and a tube of glue.

PHILIP. Darling, this glue. It's not that special quick-drying sort, is it, that you can never get unstuck . . . ? Oh, Mrs Clackett's made us some sardines.

Exit PHILIP *into the study with the tax demand, envelope, glue and one of the plates of sardines from the telephone table.*
Enter ROGER *from the bedroom, holding the hot water bottle. He looks up and down the landing.*
Enter VICKI *from the bedroom.*

VICKI. Now what?

ROGER. A hot water bottle! *I* didn't put it there!

VICKI. *I* didn't put it there.

ROGER. Someone in the bathroom, filling hot water bottles.

Exit ROGER *into the mezzanine bathroom.*

VICKI (*anxious*): You don't think there's something creepy going on?

Exit VICKI *into the mezzanine bathroom.*
Enter FLAVIA *along the upstairs corridor.*

FLAVIA. Darling, are you coming to bed or aren't you?

Exit FLAVIA *into the bedroom.*
Enter ROGER *and* VICKI *from the mezzanine bathroom.*

ROGER. What did you say?

VICKI. I didn't say anything.

ROGER. I mean, first the door handle. Now the hot water bottle . . .

VICKI. I can feel goose-pimples all over.

ROGER. Yes, quick, get something round you.

VICKI. Get the covers over our heads.

ROGER *is about to open the bedroom door.*

ROGER. Just a moment. What did I do with those sardines?

He goes downstairs. VICKI *makes to follow.*

You—wait here.

VICKI (*uneasy*): You hear all sorts of funny things about these old houses.

ROGER. Yes, but this one has been extensively modernised throughout. I can't see how anything creepy would survive oil-fired central heating and . . .

VICKI. What? What is it?

ROGER stares at the telephone table in silence.
The bedroom door opens, and FLAVIA *puts* VICKI*'s flight bag on the table outside without looking round.*
The door closes again.

VICKI. What's happening?

ROGER. The sardines. They've gone.

VICKI. Perhaps there is something funny going on. I'm going to get into bed and put my head under the . . .

She freezes at the sight of the flight bag.

ROGER. I put them there. Or was it *there?*

VICKI. Bag . . .

VICKI runs down the stairs to ROGER, *who is directly underneath the gallery.*

ROGER. I suppose Mrs Sprockett must have taken them away again . . . What? What is it?

VICKI. Bag!

ROGER. Bag?

VICKI. Bag! Bag!

Enter FLAVIA *from the bedroom with the box of files. She picks up the flight bag as well, and takes them both off along the upstairs corridor. As she does so,* VICKI *drags* ROGER *back upstairs.*

ROGER. What do you mean, bag, bag?

VICKI. Bag! Bag! Bag!

ROGER. What bag?

VICKI sees the empty table outside the bedroom door.

VICKI. No bag!

ROGER. No bag?

VICKI. Your bag! Suddenly! Here! Now—gone!

ROGER. It's in the bedroom. I put it in the bedroom.

Exit ROGER into the bedroom.

VICKI. Don't go in there!

Enter ROGER from the bedroom.

ROGER. The box!

VICKI. The box?

ROGER. They've both gone!

VICKI. Oh! My files!

ROGER. What on earth's happening? Where's Mrs Spratchett?

He starts downstairs. VICKI follows him.

You wait in the bedroom.

VICKI. No! No! No!

She runs downstairs.

ROGER. Well, get dressed, then!

VICKI. I'm not going in there!

ROGER. I'll fetch your dress out here.

Exit ROGER into the bedroom.
Enter ROGER from the bedroom.

Your dress has gone.

VICKI. Oh!

ROGER goes downstairs.

ROGER. Don't panic! Don't panic! There's some perfectly
rational explanation for all this. I'll fetch Mrs Splotchett and

she'll tell us what's happening. You wait here . . . You can't
stand here looking like that . . . You wait in the study . . .
Study, study, study!

Exit ROGER *into the service quarters.*
VICKI *opens the study door. There is a roar of exasperation
from* PHILIP, *off. She turns and flees.*

VICKI. Roger! There's something in there! Where are you?

There is another cry from PHILIP, *off.*
Exit VICKI *blindly through the front door.*
Enter PHILIP *from the study. He is holding the tax demand
in his right hand, and one of the plates of sardines in his
left.*

PHILIP. Darling, I know this is going to sound silly, but . . .

*He struggles to get the tax demand unstuck from his fingers,
encumbered by the plate of sardines.*
Enter FLAVIA *along the upstairs corridor, carrying various
pieces of bric-à-brac.*

FLAVIA. Darling, if we're not going to bed I'm going to clear
out the attic.

PHILIP. Darling, I can't come to bed! I'm glued to a tax
demand!

FLAVIA. Darling, why don't you put the sardines down?

PHILIP *puts the plate of sardines down on the table. But when
he takes his hand away the sardines come with it.*

PHILIP. Darling, I'm stuck to the sardines!

FLAVIA. Darling, don't play the fool. Get that bottle marked
poison in the downstairs loo. That eats through anything.

Exit FLAVIA *along the upstairs corridor.*

PHILIP (*flaps the tax demand*): I've heard of people getting
stuck with a *problem*, but this is ridiculous.

Exit PHILIP *into the downstairs bathroom.*

Pause.

LLOYD. Selsdon . . . ? You're on, Selsdon. We're there. The moment's arrived . . .

BELINDA (*off*): It's all right, love. He's coming, he's coming . . .

LLOYD. But there should be an arm coming through that window even before Freddie's off!

> *A pane of glass shatters in the mullioned window, and an arm comes through and releases the catch.*

LLOYD. Ah. Here it comes.

> *The window opens, and through it appears an elderly* BURGLAR. *He has great character, but is in need of extensive repair and modernisation.*
>
> BURGLAR. No bars, no burglar alarm. They ought to be prosecuted for incitement.
>
> *He climbs in.*

LLOYD. All right, Selsdon, hold it. Let's take it again.

> BURGLAR. No, but sometimes it makes me want to sit down and weep. When I think I used to do banks! When I remember I used to do bullion vaults! What am I doing now?—I'm breaking into paper bags!

LLOYD. Hold it, Selsdon. Hold it!

> *Pours himself a drink.*

LLOYD. *Hold it!*

Enter POPPY *from the wings.*

> BURGLAR. I know they're all in Spain, 'cause the old turkey in the kitchen told me so . . .

POPPY. Lloyd wants you to hold it.

Enter BELINDA.

> BURGLAR. And I know *she's* out, 'cause I've just seen her come out of the front door in her swimming costume . . .

BELINDA. Stop, Selsdon, my love! Wait, my precious!

SELSDON *stops, restrained at last by* BELINDA*'s hand on his arm.*

LLOYD. My God, it's like Myra Hess playing on through the air-raids.

SELSDON. Stop?

POPPY. Stop.

BELINDA. Stop.

LLOYD. Thank you, Belinda. Thank you, Poppy.

Exeunt BELINDA *and* POPPY.

Selsdon . . .

SELSDON. I met Myra Hess once.

LLOYD. I think he can hear better than I can.

SELSDON. I beg your pardon?

LLOYD. From your entrance, please, Selsdon.

SELSDON. Well, it was during the war, at a charity show in Sunderland . . .

LLOYD. Thank you! Poppy!

SELSDON. Oh, not for me. It stops me sleeping.

Enter POPPY *from the wings.*

LLOYD. Put the glass back, will you?

SELSDON. Come on again?

LLOYD. Right. Only, Selsdon . . .

SELSDON. Yes?

LLOYD. A little sooner, Selsdon. A shade earlier. Like *yesterday.* Freddie!

Enter FREDERICK *from the downstairs bathroom.*

(*To* SELSDON:) Start moving as soon as Freddie opens the door. (*To* FREDERICK:) What's the line?

FREDERICK. 'I've heard of people getting stuck with a *problem,* but this is ridiculous.'

LLOYD. Start moving as soon as you hear the line, 'I've heard of people getting *stuck* with a problem . . .'

FREDERICK. '*Stuck* with a problem'?

LLOYD. '*Stuck* with a problem, but this is ridiculous.' And I want your arm through that window. Right?

SELSDON. Say no more. May I make just one suggestion, though?

LLOYD. What is it, Selsdon?

SELSDON. Should I perhaps come on a little earlier?

LLOYD. Selsdon . . .

SELSDON. Only there does seem to be something of a hiatus between Freddie's exit and my entrance.

LLOYD. No, Selsdon. Listen. Don't worry. I've got it.

SELSDON. Yes?

LLOYD. How about coming on a little earlier?

SELSDON. We're obviously thinking along the same lines.

Exit SELSDON *through the window.*
Enter FREDERICK *from the downstairs bathroom.*

LLOYD. Am I putting him on or is he putting me on? Right, Freddie, from your exit.

> PHILIP (*flaps the tax demand*): I've heard of people getting *stuck* with a problem, but this is ridiculous.
>
> *Exit* PHILIP *into downstairs bathroom.*
> *Enter* BURGLAR *as before, but on time.*
>
> BURGLAR. No bars, no burglar alarms. They ought to be prosecuted for incitement.
>
> *He climbs in.*
>
> BURGLAR. No, but sometimes it makes me want to sit down and weep. When I think I used to do banks! When I remember I used to do bullion vaults! What am I doing now?—I'm breaking into paper bags!
>
> *Pours himself a drink.*

I know they're all in Spain, 'cause the old turkey in the kitchen told me so. And I know *she's* out, 'cause I've just seen her come out the front door in her swimming costume . . . Where is the front door . . . ?

Peers shortsightedly, then opens the front door ready for his departure.

Right, get the van loaded up. No rush. I've only got all flaming afternoon! Right, what are they offering? (*Peers at the television.*) One microwave oven.

Unplugs it and puts it on the sofa.

What? Fifty quid? Hardly worth lifting it.

Picks up his drink and inspects the paintings and ornaments.

Junk . . . Junk . . . If you insist . . .

Pockets some small item.

Where's his desk? No, they all say the same thing—it's hard to adjust to retirement.

Exit BURGLAR *into the study, holding his drink.*
Enter ROGER *from the service quarters, followed by* MRS
CLACKETT, *who is holding another plate of sardines.*

ROGER. . . . And the prospective tenant naturally wishes to know if there is any previous history of paranormal phenomena.

MRS CLACKETT. Oh, yes, dear, it's all nice and paranormal.

ROGER. I mean, has anything ever dematerialised before? Has anything ever flown about?

MRS CLACKETT *puts the sardines down on the telephone table, moves the television set back, plugs it in, and closes the front door.*

MRS CLACKETT. Flown about? No, the things move themselves on their own two feet, just like they do in any house.

ROGER. I'll tell the prospective tenant. She is inspecting the study.

He opens the study door and then closes it again.

There's a man in there!

MRS CLACKETT. No, no, there's no one in the house, love.

ROGER (*opens the study door*): Look! Look! He's . . . *searching* for something.

MRS CLACKETT (*glances briefly*): I can't see no one.

ROGER. You can't see him? But this is extraordinary! And where is my prospective tenant? I left her in there! She's gone! My prospective tenant has disappeared!

He closes the study door, and looks round the living room. He sees the sardines on the telephone table.

Oh my God.

MRS CLACKETT. Now what?

ROGER. There!

MRS CLACKETT. Where?

ROGER. The sardines!

MRS CLACKETT. Oh, the sardines.

ROGER. You can see the sardines, can you?

MRS CLACKETT. I can see the sardines.

ROGER *touches them cautiously, then picks up the plate.*

I can see the way they're going, too.

ROGER. I'm not letting these sardines out of my hand. But where is my prospective tenant?

He goes upstairs, holding the sardines.

MRS CLACKETT. I can see I'm going to be opening sardines all night, in and out of here like the cuckoo on a clock.

Exit MRS CLACKETT into the service quarters.

ROGER. Vicki! Vicki!

Exit ROGER into the mezzanine bathroom.

Enter BURGLAR *from the study, carrying* PHILIP'*s box and bag. He empties the contents of the box out behind the sofa, and loads the silverware into the box.*

BURGLAR. I said, 'I may be seventy, but I've still got all my wits about me.' He didn't have any answer to that.

Enter ROGER *from the bedroom, still holding the sardines.*

ROGER (*calls*): Vicki! Vicki!

Exit ROGER *into the linen cupboard.*

BURGLAR. Or if he did, *I* didn't hear it.

Exit BURGLAR *into study, not having seen or heard* ROGER. *Enter* PHILIP *from the downstairs bathroom. His right hand is still stuck to the tax demand, his left to the plate of sardines.*

PHILIP. Darling, this stuff that eats through anything. It doesn't eat through glue . . . It just eats through *trousers!* Darling, if it eats through trousers, you don't think it goes on and eats through . . . Listen, darling, I think I'd better get these trousers off! (*He begins to do so, as best he can.*) Darling, quick, this is an emergency! Have we got any stuff that stops the stuff that stops the stuff? I mean, if it eats through absolutely anything . . . Darling, I think I can feel it! I think it's eating through . . . absolutely everything!

Enter ROGER *from the linen cupboard, still holding the sardines.*

ROGER. There's something evil in this house.

PHILIP *pulls up his trousers.*

PHILIP (*aside*): The Inland Revenue!

ROGER (*frightened*): He's back!

PHILIP. No!

ROGER. No?

PHILIP. I'm not here.

ROGER. Oh my God.

PHILIP. I'm abroad.

ROGER. He's walking abroad.

PHILIP. I must go.

ROGER. Stay!

PHILIP. I'm not staying.

ROGER. Speak!

PHILIP. Only in the presence of my lawyer.

ROGER. Only in the . . . ? Hold on. Hold on. You're just an intruder, an ordinary intruder!

PHILIP. Well, nice to meet you.

Waves goodbye with his right hand, then sees the tax demand on it, and hurriedly puts it away behind his back.

I mean, have a sardine.

Offers the sardines on his left hand. His trousers, unsupported, fall down.

ROGER. No, you're not! You're some kind of sex criminal! You've done something to Vicki! I'm going to come downstairs and sort you out!

ROGER *comes downstairs and dials 999.*

PHILIP. Oh, you've got some sardines. Well, if there's nothing I can offer you . . .

ROGER (*into the phone*): Police!

PHILIP. . . . I think I'll be running along.

Runs, his trousers still round his ankles. Exit through front door.

ROGER. Come back . . . ! (*Into the phone:*) Hello—police? Someone has broken into my house! Or rather someone has broken into someone's house . . . Yes, a sex criminal! And a young woman is missing!

Enter VICKI *through the window.*

VICKI. It's in the garden now, and it's a man!

ROGER (*into the phone*): Sorry—the young woman has reappeared. (*Hand over phone:*) Are you all right?

VICKI. No, he almost saw me!

ROGER (*into the phone*): He almost saw her . . . No, but he's a burglar as well! He's taken our things!

VICKI (*finds* PHILIP's *bag and box*): The things are here.

ROGER (*into the phone*): The things have come back. So we're just missing a plate of sardines.

VICKI (*finds the sardines left near the front door by* ROGER): Here are the sardines.

ROGER (*into the phone*): And we've found the sardines.

VICKI. This is the police? You want the police here—in my underwear?

ROGER (*into the phone*): So what am I saying? I'm saying, Let's say no more about it. (*Puts the phone down.*) I thought something terrible had happened to you!

VICKI. It has! I know him!

ROGER. You know him?

VICKI. He's dealt with by our office!

ROGER. He's just an ordinary sex criminal.

VICKI. Yes, but he mustn't see me like this! You have to keep up certain standards if you work for Inland Revenue!

ROGER. Well, put something on!

VICKI. I haven't got anything!

ROGER. There must be something in the bathroom!

He picks up the box and bag and leads the way upstairs towards the mezzanine bathroom.

Bring the sardines!

Exeunt ROGER *and* VICKI *into the mezzanine bathroom.*
Enter the BURGLAR *from the study, carrying a tape-recorder.*

BURGLAR. 'What?' I said. 'When have I ever needed to run off in the middle of a job to have a Jimmy Riddle?'

Puts the tape-recorder down by the front door.

BURGLAR. 'Except when some stupid berk goes and starts talking about it . . . ?' Oh, my Gawd! Where is it?

Enter ROGER from the mezzanine bathroom, carrying the box and bag.

ROGER. Just stay in there.

Enter VICKI from the mezzanine bathroom, holding up a very short off-the-shoulder white nightdress.

ROGER. And don't come out till you've got dressed.

Exit ROGER into the bedroom.

VICKI. But I can't go around in front of our taxpayers wearing *this!*

Exit VICKI into the bedroom.

BURGLAR. I knew I shouldn't have brought the subject up.

Exit BURGLAR into the open door of the mezzanine bathroom. Enter PHILIP through the front door.

PHILIP. Darling! Help! Where are you?

Enter VICKI from the bedroom, holding the nightdress, followed by ROGER.
Exit PHILIP hurriedly into the downstairs bathroom.

ROGER. Just put it on! It's a start, at any rate! I'll find a bottom —I'll find a top—I'll find something.

Exit ROGER into the bedroom.
Exit VICKI into the mezzanine bathroom.
Enter VICKI from the mezzanine bathroom.

VICKI. Someone in there! It's *him!*

Exit VICKI hurriedly into the downstairs bathroom.
Enter FLAVIA along the upstairs corridor, carrying an old biscuit tin.

FLAVIA. Oh, darling, I'm finding such lovely things!

VICKI screams, off.

Do you remember this old biscuit tin . . .

Enter VICKI from the downstairs bathroom. She stops at the sight of FLAVIA.

. . . you gave me on the very first anniversary of our . . . ? Who are you?

VICKI. Oh my God, it's his wife and dependents!

She puts her hands over her face.
Enter PHILIP from the downstairs bathroom, still with his hands encumbered, holding the nightdress now as well, and keeping his trousers up with his elbows.

PHILIP. I've taken your dress off you!

FLAVIA gasps. PHILIP looks up at the gallery and sees her.

(*To* FLAVIA:) Where have you been? I've been going mad! Look at the state I'm in!

He holds up his hands to show FLAVIA the state he is in, and his trousers fall down.
The biscuit tin slips from FLAVIA's horrified hands, and crashes on the floor of the living room below.
PHILIP hurries towards the stairs, trousers around his ankles, hands extended in supplication.
VICKI flees before him and takes refuge in the linen cupboard.

PHILIP. Darling, I was just trying to explain to her about Inland Revenue being after us, and my fingers got stuck!

Exit FLAVIA, with a cry of pain, along the upstairs corridor.

Enter ROGER from the bedroom, directly in PHILIP's path.
PHILIP holds up the nightdress in front of his face.

ROGER. Don't keep waving that thing in my face! I'm *trying* to find something! I'll look in the other rooms.

Exit ROGER along upstairs corridor.
PHILIP turns to go back downstairs. The mezzanine lavatory flushes. He stops.

Enter the BURGLAR *from the mezzanine bathroom, holding two gold taps.*

BURGLAR. One pair gold taps, anyway . . .

He stops at the sight of PHILIP.

Oh, my Gawd!

PHILIP. Who are you?

BURGLAR. Me? Fixing the taps.

PHILIP. Tax? Income tax?

BURGLAR. That's right, governor. In come new taps—out go the old taps.

Exit BURGLAR *into the mezzanine bathroom.*

PHILIP. Tax-inspectors everywhere!

ROGER (*off*): Oh my God!

PHILIP. The other one!

Exit PHILIP *into the bedroom, holding the nightdress in front of his face.*
Enter ROGER *along the upstairs corridor.*

ROGER. Tin boxes flying about! There *is* something funny going on here! Are you dressed yet?

Exit ROGER *into mezzanine bathroom.*
Enter PHILIP *from the bedroom, trying to pull the nightdress off his head.*

PHILIP. Darling! I've got it stuck to my head now!

Enter ROGER *from the mezzanine bathroom.*
Exit PHILIP *into the bedroom.*

ROGER. A man!

Enter the BURGLAR *from the mezzanine bathroom.*

BURGLAR. Just doing the taps, governor.

ROGER. Attacks? Not attacks on women.

BURGLAR. Try anything, governor, but I'll do the taps on the bath first.

Exit BURGLAR *into the mezzanine bathroom.*

ROGER. Sex criminals everywhere! Where is Vicki? Vicki . . . ?

Exit ROGER *into the downstairs bathroom.*
Enter BURGLAR *from the mezzanine bathroom, heading for the front door.*

BURGLAR. People everywhere! I'm off. A tax on women? I don't know, they'll put a tax on anything these days.

Enter ROGER *from the downstairs bathroom. The* BURGLAR *makes a U-turn and heads back towards the mezzanine bathroom.*

ROGER. If I can't find her, you're going to be in trouble, you see.

BURGLAR. W.C.? I'll fix it.

Exit BURGLAR *into the mezzanine bathroom.*

ROGER. Vicki . . . ?

Exit ROGER *through the front door.*
Enter PHILIP *from the bedroom. The nightdress is still on his head, but is now arranged like a burnous, and he is wrapped in a white bedsheet.*
Enter VICKI *from the linen cupboard, enrobed from head to foot in a black bedsheet. They close the doors behind them. The sound makes them see each other and start back.*
Enter ROGER *through the front door.*

ROGER. Sheikh! I thought you were coming at four? And this is your charming wife? So you want to see over the house now, do you, Sheikh? Right. Well. Since you're upstairs already . . .

ROGER *goes upstairs.*
Enter FLAVIA *along the upstairs corridor, carrying a vase.*

FLAVIA. Him and his floozie! I'll break this over their heads!

ROGER. . . . let's start downstairs.

ROGER, PHILIP and VICKI go downstairs.

FLAVIA. Who are you? Who are these creatures?

ROGER (*to* PHILIP *and* VICKI): I'm sorry about this. I don't know who she is. No connection with the house, I assure you.

Enter MRS CLACKETT *from the service quarters, with another plate of sardines.* ROGER *advances to introduce her.*

Whereas this good lady with the sardines, on the other hand . . .

MRS CLACKETT. No other hands, thank you, not in my sardines, 'cause this time I'm eating them.

ROGER. . . . is fully occupied with her sardines, so perhaps the toilet facilities would be of more interest.

He ushers PHILIP *and* VICKI *away from* MRS CLACKETT *towards the mezzanine bathroom.*

FLAVIA. Mrs Clackett, who are these people?

MRS CLACKETT. Oh, we get them all the time, love. They're just Arab sheets.

ROGER. I'm sorry about this.

He opens the door to the mezzanine bathroom.

But in here . . .

FLAVIA. *Arab* sheets?

Exit FLAVIA *into the bedroom.*
Enter the BURGLAR *from the mezzanine bathroom.*

ROGER. In here we have . . .

BURGLAR. Ballcocks, governor. Your ballcocks have gone.

ROGER. Oh, we have him.

Enter FLAVIA *from the bedroom.*

FLAVIA. They're *Irish* sheets! Irish linen sheets off my own bed!

MRS CLACKETT. Oh, the thieving devils!

ROGER. In the *study*, however . . .

MRS CLACKETT. You give me that sheet, you devil!

*She seizes the nearest sheet, and it comes away in her hand
to reveal* VICKI.

Oh, and there she stands in her smalls, for all the world to
see!

ROGER. It's you!

FLAVIA. It's her!

FLAVIA *comes downstairs menacingly.*
Exit PHILIP *discreetly into the study.*

BURGLAR. It's my little girl!

VICKI. Dad!

FLAVIA *stops.*
Enter PHILIP *from the study in amazement. (He is now
played by a double.)*

BURGLAR. Our little Vicki, that ran away from home, I thought
I'd never see again!

MRS CLACKETT. Well, would you believe it?

VICKI (*to* BURGLAR): What are you doing here like this?

BURGLAR. What are *you* doing here like *that?*

VICKI. Me? I'm taking our files on tax evasion to Inland
Revenue in Basingstoke.

PHILIP *collapses behind the sofa, clutching at his heart,
unnoticed by the others.*

FLAVIA (*threateningly*): So where's my other sheet?

*Enter through the front door the most sought-after of all
properties on the market today—a* SHEIKH.
He is wearing Arab robes, and bears a strong resemblance to
PHILIP, *since he is played by the same actor.*

SHEIKH. Ah! A house of heavenly peace! I rent it!

OMNES. You!

FLAVIA. Is it?

FREDERICK. Lloyd, sorry, but I've still got my trousers round my ankles. It's just frightfully difficult doing a quick-change without a dresser.

LLOYD. Get Tim to help you. Tim! Where's Tim? Come on, Tim! Tim!

TIM, *wearing the sheet as* PHILIP's *double, gets to his feet and gazes blearily at* LLOYD.

TIM. Sorry?

LLOYD. Oh, yes. You're acting.

TIM. I must have dropped off down there.

LLOYD. Never mind, Tim.

TIM. Do something?

LLOYD. No, let it pass. We'll just struggle through on our own. Tim has a sleep behind the sofa, while all the rest of us run round with our trousers round our ankles. OK, Freddie? From your entrance, *with* trousers round ankles. 'So where's my other sheet.'

FREDERICK *hesitates*.

Some other problem, Freddie?

FREDERICK. Well, since we're stopped anyway.

LLOYD. Why did I ask?

FREDERICK. I mean, you know how stupid I am about plot.

LLOYD. I know, Freddie.

FREDERICK. May I ask another silly question?

LLOYD. All my studies in world drama are at your disposal, Freddie.

FREDERICK. I still don't understand why the Sheikh just happens to be Philip's double.

GARRY. Because he comes in and we all think he's, you know, and we all, I mean, that's the joke.

FREDERICK. I see that.

BELINDA. My sweet, the rest of the plot depends on it!

FREDERICK. I see that. But it *is* rather a coincidence, isn't it?

LLOYD. It *is* rather a coincidence, Freddie, yes. Until you reflect that there was an earlier draft of the play, now unfortunately lost to us. And in this the author makes it clear that Philip's father as a young man had travelled extensively in the Middle East.

FREDERICK. I see . . . I *see!*

LLOYD. You see?

FREDERICK. That's very interesting.

LLOYD. I thought you'd like that.

FREDERICK. But will the audience get it?

LLOYD. You must tell them, Freddie. Looks. Gestures. That's what acting's all about. OK?

FREDERICK. Yes. Thank you, Lloyd. Thank you.

LLOYD. Right, can we just finish the act? From your entrance, Freddie.

Exit PHILIP *through the front door.*

God, I'm being so clever out here! What's going to be left of this show when I've gone back to London and you're up there on your own? 'So where's my other sheet?'

FLAVIA (*threateningly*): So where's my other sheet?

Enter the SHEIKH *through the front door.*

SHEIKH. Ah! A house of heavenly peace! I rent it!

OMNES. You!

FLAVIA. Is it?

SHEIKH (*with dignity*): Is me? Certainly is me! Who else?

They all fall upon him.

ROGER. You walk in asking to view a house like this, when you're nothing but a trouserless tramp! (*He pulls up the* SHEIKH's *robes.*)

SHEIKH. What?

MRS CLACKETT. You take all the clean sheets! (*Tries to pull the robes off him.*)

VICKI. You snatch my nightdress! (*Tries to pull his burnous off him.*)

SHEIKH. What? What?

FLAVIA. You toss me aside like a broken china doll! (*She hits him.*)

SHEIKH. What? What? What?

BURGLAR. And what you're up to with my little girl down there in Basingstoke I won't ask. But I'll tell you one thing, Vicki.

Pause.

LLOYD. Brooke!

BROOKE. Sorry . . .

LLOYD. Your line. Come on, love, we're two lines away from the end of the act.

BROOKE. I don't understand.

LLOYD. Give her the line!

BELINDA (*to* BROOKE): 'What's that, Dad?'

BROOKE. Yes, but I don't understand.

DOTTY. It's 'What's that, Dad?'

SELSDON. Yes, I say to you, 'I'll tell you one thing, Vicki,' and you say to me, 'What's that, Dad?'

BROOKE. I don't understand why the Sheikh looks like Philip.

Silence. Everyone waits for the storm.

LLOYD. Poppy! Bring the book!

Enter POPPY *from the wings, with the book.*

Is that the line, Poppy? 'I don't understand why the Sheikh looks like Philip?' Can we consult the author's text, and make absolutely sure?

POPPY. Well, I think it's . . .

LLOYD (*comes up on stage*): 'What's that, Dad?' Right. That's the line, Brooke, love. We all know you've worked in very classy places up in London where they let you make the play up as you go along, but we don't want that kind of thing here, love, not when the author has provided us with such a considered and polished line of his own, not at one o'clock in the morning, not two lines away from the end of Act One, not when we're just about to get a tea-break before we all drop dead of exhaustion. We merely want to hear the line, 'What's that, Dad?' That's all. Nothing else. I'm not being unreasonable, am I?

BROOKE *abruptly turns, runs upstairs, and exits into the mezzanine bathroom.*

Exit? Does it say 'exit'?

The sound of BROOKE *weeping, off, and running downstairs.*

Oh God, now she's going to wash her lenses away.

Exit LLOYD *through the front door.*

FREDERICK (*chastened*): Oh dear.

SELSDON (*likewise*): A little heavy with the sauce, I thought.

GARRY. I thought it was going to be Poppy when he finally, you know.

DOTTY. It's usually Poppy. Isn't it, love?

POPPY *smiles wryly.*

FREDERICK. I suppose that was all my fault.

GARRY. But why pick on, you know?

DOTTY. Yes, why Brooke?

BELINDA. I thought it was quite sweet, actually.

GARRY. Sweet?

BELINDA. A little lovers' tiff, really.

DOTTY. What, you mean, Lloyd and Brooke . . . ?

BELINDA. Didn't you know?

SELSDON. Brooke and Lloyd?

BELINDA. Where do you think they've been all weekend?

FREDERICK. Good God. You mean, that's why he didn't realise they'd put the set up wrong on Sunday . . . ?

BELINDA. Sh! Here they come!

Enter LLOYD *with his arm round* BROOKE.

LLOYD. OK. All forgotten. I was irresistible.

POPPY. I think I'm going to be sick.

Exit POPPY *into the wings.*

LLOYD. What?

DOTTY. Oh, no!

LLOYD. Oh, God!

Exit LLOYD *after* POPPY.

GARRY. You mean . . . ?

SELSDON. Her, too?

FREDERICK. Oh, dear.

BELINDA. Well, that's something I *didn't* know.

BROOKE. I think I'm going to faint.

DOTTY. Yes, sit down, love!

BELINDA. Head between your knees, my precious.

They sit BROOKE *down with her head between her knees.*

SELSDON. Well, that's something *she* didn't know!

BELINDA. Hush, love.

DOTTY. Two weeks' rehearsal, that's all we've had.

FREDERICK. Whatever next?

SELSDON. *Most* exciting!

BELINDA. Sh! (*Indicates* BROOKE.)

SELSDON. Oh, yes. Sh!

DOTTY. Here he comes.

Enter LLOYD *from the wings, subdued.*

Is she all right, love?

LLOYD. She'll be all right in a minute. Something she ate, probably.

GARRY (*indicates* BROOKE): Yes, this one's feeling a bit, you know.

LLOYD. I'm feeling a bit, you know, myself. I think I'm going to . . .

BELINDA. Which?

GARRY (*offers chair*): Faint?

BELINDA (*offers vase*): Or be sick?

LLOYD. . . . Need that tea-break.

DOTTY. You're certainly overdoing it at the moment, love.

LLOYD. So could we just have the last line of the act?

SELSDON. Me? Last line? Right. 'But I'll tell you one thing, Vicki.'

> VICKI. What's that, Dad?
>
> BURGLAR. When all around is strife and uncertainty, there's nothing like . . .
>
> *He takes* MRS CLACKETT's *plate.*
>
> . . . a good old-fashioned plate of sardines!

LLOYD. And *curtain!*

Pause. Then TIM *realises, and hobbles hurriedly into the wings.*

Curtain.

Act Two

II

ACT ONE

> *The living-room of the Brents' country home. Wednesday afternoon. (Theatre Royal, Goole. Wednesday matinee, February 13.)*

But this time we are watching the act from behind; the whole set has been turned through 180 degrees. All the doors can be seen—there is no masking behind them. Two stairways lead up to the platform which gives access to the doors on the upper levels. Some of the scene inside the living-room is visible through the full-length window. There are also two doors in the backstage fabric of the theatre: one giving access to the dressing-rooms, and the pass door into the auditorium. TIM *is walking up and down anxiously in his dinner jacket.* POPPY *is speaking into the microphone in the prompt corner.*

POPPY (*over the Tannoy*): Act One beginners, please. Your calls, Miss Otley, Miss Ashton, Mr Lejeune, Mr Fellowes, Miss Blair. Act One beginners, please.

TIM. And maybe Act One beginners is what we'll get. What do you think?

POPPY (*to* TIM): Oh, she'll pull herself together now we've called Beginners. Now she knows she's got to be on stage in five minutes. Won't she?

TIM. Will she?

POPPY. You know what Dotty's like.

TIM. We've only been on the road for a month! We've only got to Goole! What's it going to be like by the time we've got to Stockton-on-Tees?

POPPY. If only she'd speak!

TIM. If only she'd unlock the door! Look, if Dotty *won't* go on . . .

POPPY. Won't go on?

TIM. *If* she won't.

POPPY. She will.

TIM. Of course she will.

POPPY. Won't she?

TIM. I'm sure she will. But if she *doesn't* . . .

POPPY. She must!

TIM. She will, she will. But if she *didn't* . . .

POPPY. I'd have five minutes to change. Four minutes.

TIM. If only she'd say something.

The pass door opens cautiously, and LLOYD *puts his head round. He closes it again at the sight of* POPPY.

POPPY. I'll have another go. Takes your mind off your own problems, anyway.

Exit POPPY *in the direction of the dressing-rooms.*
LLOYD *puts his head back round the door.*

LLOYD. Has she gone?

TIM. Lloyd! I didn't know you were coming down today!

LLOYD *comes in. He is carrying a bottle of whisky.*

LLOYD. I wasn't. I haven't.

TIM. Anyway, thank God you're here!

LLOYD. I'm not.

TIM. Dotty and Garry . . .

LLOYD. I don't want anyone to know I'm in.

TIM. No, but Dotty and Garry . . .

LLOYD (*gives him the bottle*): Hide this somewhere.

TIM. Right. They've had some kind of row . . .

LLOYD (*takes money out of wallet and gives it to* TIM). There's a flower shop just across the road at the back. I want you to buy me some very large and expensive looking flowers.

TIM. Right. Now Dotty's locked herself up in her dressing-room.

LLOYD. Don't let Poppy see them.

TIM. No. And she won't speak to anyone . . .

LLOYD. First house finishes just after five, yes? Second house starts at seven-thirty? I want two hours alone and undisturbed with Brooke in her dressing-room between the shows, then I'm on the 7.25 back to London.

TIM. Lloyd, that's what I'm trying to tell you—there may not *be* a show!

LLOYD. She hasn't walked out already?

TIM. No one knows what she's doing! She's locked in her dressing-room! She won't speak to anyone!

LLOYD. You've called Beginners?

TIM. Yes!

LLOYD. I can't do it in five minutes. It's not physiologically possible.

TIM. She's had bust-ups with Garry before, of course.

LLOYD. Brooke's had a bust-up with *Garry?*

TIM. Brooke? Not Brooke—Dotty!

LLOYD. Oh, Dotty.

TIM. I mean, they had the famous bust-up the week before last, when we were playing Worksop.

LLOYD. Right, right, you told me on the phone.

TIM. She went out with this journalist bloke . . .

LLOYD. Journalist—yes, yes . . .

TIM. But you know Garry threatened to kill him?

LLOYD. Killed him, yes, I know. Listen, don't worry about Dotty—she's got money in the show.

TIM. Yes, but now it's happened again! Two o'clock this morning I'm woken up by this great banging on my door. It's Garry. Do I know where Dotty is?—She hasn't come home.

LLOYD. Tim, let me tell you something about *my* life. I have the Duke of Buckingham on the phone to me for an hour after rehearsal every evening complaining that the Duke of Gloucester is sucking boiled sweets through his speeches. Catesby is off every afternoon doing a telly, and the Duke of Clarence is off for the entire week doing a commercial for Madeira. Richard himself—would you believe?—Richard III has now gone down with a back problem. Then last night Brooke rings me to say she's very unhappy here, and she's got herself a doctor's certificate for nervous exhaustion. I have no time to find or rehearse another Vicki. I have just one afternoon, while Richard is fitted for a surgical corset and Lady Anne starts divorce proceedings, to cure Brooke of nervous exhaustion, with no medical aids except a little whisky—you've got the whisky?—a few flowers—don't forget to put the flowers in water—and a certain fading bedside manner. So I haven't come to the theatre to hear about other people's problems. I've come to be taken out of myself, and preferably not put back again.

TIM. Yes, but Lloyd . . .

LLOYD. Have you done the front of house calls?

TIM. Oh, the front of house calls!

TIM hurries to the microphone in the prompt corner, still holding the money and whisky. He puts the whisky down to switch on the microphone.

LLOYD. And don't let Poppy see those flowers!

Exit LLOYD through the pass door.

TIM (*into microphone*): Ladies and gentlemen, will you please take your seats. The curtain will rise in three minutes.

Enter POPPY from the dressing-rooms.

POPPY. We're going to be so late up!

TIM. No luck?

POPPY. Belinda's having a go. I haven't even started the front of house calls yet . . . Money? Is this for me?

TIM. No, no! (*He puts the money behind his back and automatically produces the whisky with his other hand.*)

POPPY. Whisky!

TIM. Oh . . . Is it?

POPPY. Where did you find that?

TIM. Well . . .

POPPY. Not up here? Oh, my God, he's hiding them up here now! (*She takes the whisky.*) I'll put it downstairs where he won't find it.

Enter BELINDA *from the dressing-rooms.*

No?

BELINDA. You know what Dotty's like when she's like this. Freddie's trying now . . . (*She sees the whisky.*) Oh, my God.

POPPY. He's hiding them up here now.

Enter FREDERICK *from the dressing-rooms.*

No?

FREDERICK. No.

BELINDA. You didn't try for very long, my precious!

FREDERICK. No, well . . . (*He sees the whisky.*) Oh dear.

BELINDA. He's hiding them up here now.

Exit POPPY *to the dressing-rooms, holding the whiskey.*

No, Garry came rushing out of his dressing-room in a great state. I couldn't quite understand what he was saying. I often feel with Garry that I must have missed something somewhere. You know how stupid I am about that kind of thing. But I think he was saying he wanted to kill me.

BELINDA. Oh, my poor sweet!

FREDERICK. I thought I'd better leave him to it. I don't want to make things worse. He's all right, is he?

BELINDA. Who, Garry? Anything but, by the sound of it!

FREDERICK. I mean, he's going on?

TIM. Garry? *Garry's* going on. Of course he's going on. What's all this about Garry not going on?

BELINDA. Yes, because if you have to go on for Garry, Poppy can't go on for Dotty, because if Poppy goes on for Dotty, you'll have to be on the corner!

TIM. Oh my God.

He taps his left hand anxiously with the money in his right.

BELINDA. Money.

TIM. Money?

BELINDA. Is that for us?

TIM. No, that's for . . . oh, my God!

Exit TIM *to the dressing-rooms.*

FREDERICK. She's a funny woman, you know—Dotty. So up and down. She was perfectly all right last night.

BELINDA. Last night?

FREDERICK. Yes, she took me for a drink after the show in some club she knows about.

BELINDA. She was with *you? You* were with *her?*

FREDERICK. She was being very sympathetic about all my troubles.

BELINDA. She's not going to sink her teeth into you. I won't let her.

FREDERICK. No, no, she couldn't have been nicer. In fact she came back to my digs afterwards for a cup of tea, and she told me all *her* troubles. Sat there until three o'clock this morning—I don't know what the landlady thought!

Enter POPPY.

POPPY. And another thing.

BELINDA. Nothing else, my sweet!

POPPY. Where's Selsdon?

BELINDA. It turns out that it's Freddie here who's the cause of all the . . . Selsdon?

POPPY. He's not in his dressing-room.

BELINDA. Oh my God!

POPPY. Oh my God, the front of house calls!

BELINDA. You do the calls. I'll look for Selsdon.

FREDERICK. What shall *I* do?

BELINDA (*firmly*): Absolutely nothing at all.

FREDERICK. Right.

BELINDA. You've done quite enough already, my pet.

Exit BELINDA *to the dressing-rooms.*

POPPY (*into the microphone*): Ladies and gentlemen, will you please take your seats. The curtain will rise in three minutes.

Enter TIM *from the dressing-rooms, carrying a large bunch of flowers.*

TIM. He wants to kill someone.

POPPY. *Selsdon* wants to kill someone?

TIM. Garry, Garry . . . Selsdon?

POPPY. We've lost him.

TIM. Oh my God.

POPPY. I'll look in the pub. (*She gives the flowers to* FREDERICK.) Hold these.

Exit POPPY *to the dressing-rooms.*

TIM. I'll take that. (*Takes the flowers.*) Oh, the front of house calls! Hold this. (*Gives the flowers back to* FREDERICK.)

FREDERICK. Oh, I think Poppy's done them.

TIM. She gave them two minutes, did she? I'll give them one minute. (*Into the microphone.*) Ladies and gentlemen, will you please take your seats. The curtain will rise in one minute.

Takes the flowers from FREDERICK.

FREDERICK. Oh dear, I think she said three minutes.

TIM. *Three* minutes? *I* said three minutes! *She* said three minutes?

FREDERICK. I think so.

TIM. Hold this. (*Gives* FREDERICK *the flowers. Into microphone.*) Ladies and gentlemen, will you please take your seats. The curtain will rise in two minutes.

Enter BELINDA *from the dressing-rooms, holding the bottle of whisky.*

FREDERICK. Any luck?

BELINDA. No, but I found this.

FREDERICK. Oh dear.

TIM. Oh . . .

BELINDA. It was quite cunningly hidden behind the fire-extinguishers.

FREDERICK. *Not* a good sign.

TIM. I'll take it.

BELINDA. Yes, and put it somewhere out of sight, my sweet!

Enter POPPY *from the dressing-rooms.* TIM *conceals the whiskey from her.*

POPPY. He's not in the pub.

TIM. You've checked the green room?

BELINDA. Yes.

TIM. I'll check it again.

Exit TIM *to the dressing-rooms, with the whisky.*

BELINDA. Now what?

POPPY (*into the microphone*): Ladies and gentlemen, will you please take your seats. The curtain will rise in two minutes.

FREDERICK. Oh dear. Tim's already told them two minutes.

POPPY. He's done two minutes? (*Into the microphone.*) Ladies and gentlemen, will you please take your seats. The curtain will rise in one minute.

Enter LLOYD *through the pass door.*

LLOYD. What the fuck is going on?

BELINDA. Lloyd!

FREDERICK. Great Scott!

POPPY. I didn't know you were here!

LLOYD. I'm *not* here! I'm in London! But I can't sit out there and listen to 'two minutes'—'three minutes'—'one minute'—'two minutes'!

BELINDA. My sweet, we're having great dramas downstairs!

LLOYD. We're having great dramas out there! (*To* POPPY:) This is the matinee, honey! There's old-age pensioners out there! 'The curtain will rise in three minutes'—we all start for the Gents. 'The curtain will rise in one minute'—we all come running out again. We don't know *which* way we're going!

POPPY. Lloyd, I've got to have a talk to you.

LLOYD (*kisses her mechanically*): Just tell me one thing, honey.

POPPY. I tried phoning you.

LLOYD. Is Brooke going on?

BELINDA. Is *Brooke* going on?

Enter BROOKE *from the dressing-rooms, with the whisky.*

Brooke! You're going on, aren't you?

BROOKE. Sorry?

FREDERICK. Are you all right, Brooke?

BROOKE. Am I all right?

LLOYD. Fine. OK. She sounds like her usual self to me.

BROOKE. Lloyd?

LLOYD (*kisses her, and sees the whisky*): What's this?

BELINDA. Another one?

BROOKE. I was lying on the floor of the green room . . .

LLOYD. You were lying on the floor of the green room?

BELINDA. For her relaxation.

LLOYD. Oh yes.

BROOKE. And I saw it hidden behind the radiator.

BELINDA. Oh my God, he's hiding them everywhere!

FREDERICK (*takes the whisky*): I'll put it where he won't find it.

LLOYD. Put it in Brooke's dressing-room. He won't think of looking in . . . (*Sees the flowers that* FREDERICK *is holding.*) What's *this?*

FREDERICK. Oh, yes, sorry. (*He gives the flowers to* POPPY.)

POPPY. Tim bought them for me. (*She puts them on her desk in the prompt corner.*)

LLOYD. *Tim? Bought* them for you?

POPPY. Lloyd, there's something I've got to tell you.

LLOYD. I've heard everything I want to hear for today. (*Goes towards the pass door.*)

BELINDA. But what about Dotty?

LLOYD. No.

FREDERICK. And Garry?

LLOYD. No.

BELINDA. What about Selsdon?

LLOYD. Listen, I think this show is beyond the help of a director. You just do it. I'll sit out there in the dark with a bag of toffees and enjoy it. OK? 'One minute' was the last call, if your memory goes back that far.

Exit LLOYD *through the pass door.*
BROOKE *lies down on the floor.*

FREDERICK. *Is* she all right?

BELINDA. It's her relaxation, my precious. (*To* BROOKE:) You *are* all right, aren't you, my love?

BROOKE. Yes. I couldn't concentrate downstairs. Everyone seemed to be shouting and running around somehow.

BELINDA (*to* FREDERICK): It's her breathing, you see.

FREDERICK. Oh dear. (*To* BROOKE:) You don't have to go on, you know, if you're not feeling up to it. It's only the matinee. I'm sure Poppy would always be delighted to have a bash on your behalf. Wouldn't you, Poppy?

POPPY. I'll see what's happening downstairs.

Exit POPPY *to the dressing-rooms.*

BELINDA. Freddie, my sweet precious . . .

FREDERICK. What? Did I say something wrong?

Enter SELSDON *hurriedly through the pass door.*

SELSDON. Where's Tim?

BELINDA. Selsdon! My sweet! Where have you been?

FREDERICK. Are you all right? (*Puts out a sympathetic hand, then realises that it contains the whisky bottle.*) Oh dear. (*Hurriedly puts it out of sight behind his back.*)

BELINDA. We've been looking for you everywhere!

SELSDON. Oh, yes, everywhere. In front—manager's office—bar—not a sign of him.

BELINDA. He's looking for you, downstairs.

SELSDON. That's right! Great shindig been going on down there. I thought Tim ought to know about it.

BELINDA. My love, I think he's heard.

SELSDON. Oh, everything! Oh, he really went for her! 'I know when you've got your eye on someone!' he says. 'I've seen the way you've been looking at Teddy.'

BELINDA. Oh my God.

FREDERICK. Teddy? Who's Teddy?

BELINDA. Oh, Freddie, can't you guess?

FREDERICK. Teddy?

SELSDON. Or it may have been Neddy.

BELINDA. Oh, poor Neddy!

SELSDON. Yes, Teddy or Neddy. One of the two. Anyway . . .

Enter POPPY *from the dressing-rooms.*

POPPY. I think they're coming.

BELINDA. They're coming!

FREDERICK. They're coming!

SELSDON. I knew they wouldn't.

POPPY. And you're *here!*

SELSDON. Oh, yes, every word!

POPPY. Right. (*Into the microphone.*) Ladies and gentlemen, will you please take your seats. The performance is just about to begin.

Enter TIM *from the dressing-rooms.*

TIM. They're coming.

BELINDA. And we've found Selsdon.

TIM (*to* SELSDON): How did you get here?

SELSDON. How?

TIM (*into microphone*): Ladies and gentlemen, will you please take your seats.

POPPY. I've done it, I've done it!

TIM (*into microphone*): The performance is . . . oh.

BELINDA. Poor Lloyd! He'll choke on his toffees.

SELSDON. You want to know how? Amiss, that's how!

TIM. What?

SELSDON. How did she take it? In one word? Amiss! 'It's always the same thing,' she cries.

Enter GARRY *from the dressing-rooms.*

BELINDA. Garry, my sweet!

SELSDON. 'You try to give some poor devil a leg up.' Or she may have said, 'a leg over . . .' Oh, and here he is.

FREDERICK (*to* GARRY): Are you all right?

FREDERICK *collects the box and flight bag from the props table, and offers them to* GARRY, *who snatches them angrily.*

SELSDON. What does he say?

BELINDA. He's not saying anything, Selsdon, my sweet.

SELSDON. Very sensible. Only stir it up again. 'I've seen you at it!'— that's what he kept saying downstairs.

Enter DOTTY *from the dressing-rooms.*

'I know when you've got your claws into someone,' he says, 'and you've got them into poor old Neddy!'

BELINDA. Dotty, my love!

SELSDON. Oh, she's emerged, has she? Come on, old girl! You're on!

FREDERICK. Are you all right?

SELSDON. Is she all right?

DOTTY *merely sighs, and smiles, and gives a little squeeze of the arm to* BELINDA. *She takes up her place by the service quarters entrance, a tragically misunderstood woman.* GARRY *moves pointedly away.*

BELINDA (*to* SELSDON): She's fine.

TIM. All right, everyone?

SELSDON. Or maybe it was Eddy. Neddy or Eddy—one of the two.

BELINDA. Hush, love.

POPPY. Curtain up?

Everyone looks anxiously from DOTTY *to* GARRY *and back again.*
DOTTY *and* GARRY *both ignore the looks. They stand aloof, then
both, at the same moment, turn to check their appearance in the
little mirrors fixed to the back of the set.*

FREDERICK. Look, Dotty—look, Garry—I'm not going to make a
great speech, but we *have* all got to go out there and put on a
performance, and, well . . .

BELINDA. We can't do it in silence, my loves! We're going to have
to speak to each other!

Pause. Neither GARRY *nor* DOTTY *has apparently heard.*

DOTTY (*suddenly, to* TIM): What's the house like?

BELINDA. That's the spirit!

FREDERICK. Well done, Dotty!

TIM. It's quite good. Well, for a matinee.

POPPY. There's quite a crowd at the front of the back stalls.

SELSDON (*to* POPPY): Come on, girl, get the tabs up! Some of those
OAPs out there haven't got long to go.

POPPY. Right. Quiet, then, please . . .

FREDERICK. Let me just say one word . . . Hold it a moment,
Poppy . . .

SELSDON. Let *me* just say one word. Sardines!

BELINDA. Sardines!

FREDERICK. Sardines!

BELINDA *rushes to the prop table to fetch* DOTTY *the plate of
sardines that she takes on for her first entrance.*

POPPY (*over Tannoy*): Quiet on stage. House lights going down. Act
One . . .

Enter LLOYD *through the pass door.*

LLOYD. *Now* what?

TIM. We're just going up.

LLOYD. We've been sitting there for an hour! They've gone quiet! They think someone's died!

FREDERICK. I'm sorry, Lloyd. It's my fault. I was just saying a few words to everyone.

LLOYD. Freddie, have you ever thought of having a brain transplant?

FREDERICK. Sorry, sorry. Wrong moment. I see that.

LLOYD. Anybody else have thoughts they feel they must communicate?

POPPY. Well, not now, of course, but . . .

LLOYD. *What?*

POPPY. I mean, you know, later . . .

LLOYD (*to* TIM). And you bought those flowers for Poppy?

TIM. No . . . well . . . yes . . .

LLOYD. And you didn't buy any flowers for me?

TIM. No . . . well . . . no . . .

LLOYD. Tim, have you ever heard of such a thing as jealous rage?

TIM. Yes . . . well . . . yes . . .

LLOYD. Then take five pounds of your own money, Tim, and go out to the florists and buy some flowers for *me!* Gave Poppy the flowers! You two could have Freddie's old brain—you could have half each.

Exit LLOYD *through the pass door.*

FREDERICK. Oh dear.

BELINDA. Don't cry, Poppy, love.

SELSDON. Just get the old bus on the road.

POPPY (*over Tannoy*): Act One. Curtain up.

She presses a buzzer, and the act begins. (Note: the act that follows is a somewhat condensed version of the one we saw rehearsed.)

As the curtain rises, the award-winning modern telephone is ringing.

DOTTY *makes her entrance.*
There is a sound of scattered applause.

Enter from the service quarters MRS CLACKETT, *a housekeeper of character. She is carrying an imposing plate of sardines.*

SELSDON, BELINDA *and* FREDERICK *express silent relief that the show has at last started. They subside on to the chairs.*

MRS CLACKETT. It's no good you going on. I can't open sardines *and* answer the phone. I've only got one pair of hands. (*She puts the sardines on the telephone table by the sofa, and picks up the phone.*) Hello . . . Yes, but there's no one here, love . . . No, Mr Brent's not here . . . He lives here, yes, but he don't live here now because he lives in Spain . . . Mr Philip Brent, that's right . . . The one that writes the plays, that's him, only now he writes them in Spain . . . No, she's in Spain, too, they're all in Spain, there's no one here . . . Am I in Spain? No, I'm not in Spain, dear. I look after the house for them, only I go home at one o'clock on Wednesday, so that's where *I* am . . . No, because I've got a nice plate of sardines to put my feet up with, and they've got colour here, and it's the royal what's it called

TIM *takes his wallet and checks his money. He goes to exit, but stops and turns when* BELINDA *points out to the others* GARRY *sighing heavily as he waits for his entrance.* FREDERICK *puts the whisky down on his chair and goes across to* GARRY. BELINDA *and* TIM *watch apprehensively as* FREDERICK *gives* GARRY's *arm a silently sympathetic squeeze.*

GARRY *shakes him off indignantly.*

BELINDA *hurries across
to draw* FREDERICK *off.*
TIM *watches, flowers in
hand.* FREDERICK *cannot
understand what he has
done to cause offence. He
demonstrates what he did
by giving* GARRY'S *arm
another squeeze.*

GARRY *drops his props
and threatens to hit*
FREDERICK.

FREDERICK *covers his nose.*
BELINDA *and* TIM *separate
them, and urge* GARRY
back to the front door.
TIM *goes off toward
the dressing room.*

—the royal you know—
where's the paper, then . . . ?

*She searches in the
newspaper.*

. . . And if it's to do with
letting the house then you'll
have to ring the house-
agents, because they're the
agents for the house . . .
Squire, Squire, Hackham
and who's the other one . . . ?
No, they're not in Spain,
they're next to the phone
in the study. Squire, Squire,
Hackham, and hold on, I'll
go and look.

She replaces the receiver.

Always the same, isn't it.
Soon as you take the weight
off your feet, down it all
comes on your head.

Exit MRS CLACKETT
*into the study, still holding
the newspaper.
The sound of a key in the
lock. The front door opens.
On the doorstep stands*
ROGER, *holding a card-
board box. He is about
thirty, and has the well-
appointed air of a man who
handles high-class real
estate.*

ROGER. . . . my housekeeper,
yes, but this is her afternoon
off.

BROOKE *makes her*
entrance.

Enter VICKI *through the*
front door. She is a
desirable property in her
early twenties, well-built
and beautifully maintained
throughout.

FREDERICK *gives* DOTTY
a sympathetic squeeze of
the arm in her turn.

ROGER. So we've got the
place entirely to ourselves.

As GARRY *turns back to*
collect the flight bag he
gets a fleeting glimpse
of this.

ROGER *goes back and*
brings in a flight bag, and
closes the front door.

I'll just check.

As GARRY *comes through*
the service quarters door he
sees BELINDA *glancing at*
him and hurriedly discon-
necting FREDERICK
from DOTTY. *He stamps on*
FREDERICK'*s foot.*

He opens the door to the
service quarters. VICKI
gazes round.

Hello? Anyone at home?

FREDERICK *turns to*
BELINDA *and asks her*
what's wrong. She finds it
difficult to explain with
DOTTY *there.*

Closes the door.

No, there's no one here. So
what do you think?

VICKI. All these doors.

ROGER. Oh, only a handful,
really. Study. Kitchens, and
a self-contained service flat
for the housekeeper.

BELINDA *discovers that*
DOTTY *is now silently*
pouring out her grievances
against GARRY *to the*
sympathetic FREDERICK.

VICKI. Terrific. And which
one's the . . . ?

ROGER. What?

VICKI. You know . . .

ROGER. Oh. Through here.

Amy Wright, Dorothy Loudon

Amy Wright, Deborah Rush, Brian Murray, Dorothy Loudon, Jim Piddock

Victor Garber, Paxton Whitehead, Linda Thorson

Paxton Whitehead, Deborah Rush, Victor Garber, Amy Wright,
Douglas Seale, Linda Thorson, Jim Piddock

photos: ©1983 by Martha Swope

Opens the downstairs bathroom for her.

VICKI. Fantastic.

Exit VICKI *into the bathroom.*
Enter MRS CLACKETT *from the study, without the newspaper.*

MRS CLACKETT. Now I've lost the sardines . . .

Mutual surprise. ROGER *closes the door to the bathroom, and slips the champagne back into the bag.*

BELINDA *only just manages to detach* DOTTY *and get her back on stage for her entrance.*

ROGER. I'm sorry. I thought there was no one here.

BELINDA *tries to explain to* FREDERICK *that* DOTTY *has taken a fancy to him.* FREDERICK *can't understand a word of it. She turns to* BROOKE *to ask her to explain to* FREDERICK *but she can't understand anything.*

MRS CLACKETT. I'm not here. I'm off, only it's the royal you know, where they wear those hats, and they're all covered in fruit.

ROGER. I'm from the agents. I just dropped in to . . . go into a few things. Well, to check some of the measurements. Do one or two odd jobs.

The bathroom door opens. ROGER *closes it.*

Oh, and a client. I'm showing a prospective tenant over the house.

BELINDA *suddenly points out that* SELSDON

VICKI (*off, opening the door*): What's wrong with this door?

has discovered the whisky
that FREDERICK *left on*
the chair. SELSDON
opens the bottle, smells it,
closes it again, and then
goes off to the dressing-
rooms with it.
FREDERICK *goes to run*
after SELSDON. BELINDA
tells him to wait there—
sit still—do absolutely
nothing—while she runs
after SELSDON.
Exit BELINDA *in the*
direction of the dressing-
rooms in pursuit of
SELSDON.

DOTTY *makes her exit,*
puts down the sardines,
shaking her head with
misery, and begins to
weep.

FREDERICK *is very*
agitated by this. He takes
the sardines away from
her, pats her on the
shoulder, gives her a hand-
kerchief, pushes the

ROGER. She's thinking of
renting it. Her interest is
definitely aroused.

Enter VICKI *from*
bathroom.

VICKI. That's not the
bedroom.

ROGER. The bedroom? No,
that's the downstairs
bathroom and WC suite.
And this is the housekeeper.
Mrs Crockett.

MRS CLACKETT. Clackett,
dear, Clackett. Only now
I've lost the newspaper.

Exit MRS CLACKETT
into the study, carrying
the sardines.

ROGER. I'm sorry about this.

VICKI. That's all right. We
don't want the television,
do we?

ROGER. Only she's been in
the family for generations.

VICKI. Great. Come on, then.
(*Starts upstairs.*) I've got
to be in Basingstoke by
four.

ROGER. Perhaps we should
just have a glass of
champagne.

VICKI. We'll take it up with
us.

sardines back into her
hand, and edges her towards
the door. *At the last
moment she realises she
hasn't got the newspaper.*
FREDERICK *runs and
fetches it from the props
table. Then she realises
that she has still got the
sardines.*

*He gets them off her just
in time for her to make
her entrance.*

Enter BELINDA *from the
dressing-rooms leading a
bewildered* SELSDON, *but
without the whisky.*
FREDERICK *tells her what
a terrible state* DOTTY *is
in.*

ROGER. Yes. Well . . .

VICKI. And don't let my files
out of sight.

ROGER. No. Only . . .

VICKI. What?

ROGER. Well . . .

VICKI. Her?

ROGER. She has been in the
family for generations.

Enter MRS CLACKETT
*from the study, with the
newspaper but without the
sardines.*

MRS CLACKETT. Sardines . . .
sardines . . . It's not for me
to say, of course, dear,
only I will just say this:
don't think twice about
it—take the plunge. You'll
really enjoy it here.

VICKI. Oh. Great.

MRS CLACKETT (*to* ROGER):
Won't she, love?

ROGER. Yes. Well. Yes!

MRS CLACKETT (*to* VICKI):
And we'll enjoy having you.
(*To* ROGER:) Won't we, love?

ROGER. Oh. Well.

VICKI. Terrific.

*They turn to watch her
anxiously as she makes
her exit.*

MRS CLACKETT. Sardines,
sardines. Can't put your
feet up on an empty
stomach, can you.

Exit MRS CLACKETT *to
service quarters.*

SELSDON *seizes the
opportunity to depart
again to the dressing-
rooms.*

VICKI. You see? She thinks
it's great. She's even making
us sardines!

ROGER. Well . . .

BELINDA *runs after him.*
FREDERICK *goes to
accompany her, but turns
anxiously back to reassure*
DOTTY.

VICKI. I think she's terrific.

ROGER. Terrific.

*But she is now smiling
bravely, and telling him
that she has pulled her-
self together, thanks to
him.*
DOTTY *gives* FREDERICK
*a kiss to express her
gratitude.*

VICKI. So which way?

ROGER (*picks up the bags*):
All right. Before she comes
back with the sardines.

VICKI. Up here?

ROGER. Yes, yes.

VICKI. In here?

ROGER. Yes, yes, yes.

As GARRY *comes through
door of mezzanine bath-
room, he catches a fleeting
glimpse of the kiss.*

Exeunt ROGER *and* VICKI
into mezzanine bathroom.

VICKI. It's another bathroom.

They reappear.

*FREDERICK *now realises
that he has an entrance
coming up with* BELINDA,
and no BELINDA. *He
urgently tries to persuade*
DOTTY *to go off and find
her.*

ROGER. No, no, no.

VICKI. Always trying to get
me into bathrooms.

ROGER. I mean in *here.*

*Nods at the next door—
the first along the gallery.*

GARRY *appears in the
linen cupboard doorway
and takes a good look at
the earnest colloquy
between* FREDERICK
and DOTTY. *He throws
the sheet at them.*

VICKI *leads the way in.*
ROGER *follows.*

VICKI. Oh, black sheets!
(*Produces one.*)

ROGER. It's the airing
cupboard. (*Throws the
sheet back.*) This one, this
one, this one.

*He drops the bag and box,
and struggles nervously to
open the second door
along the gallery, the
bedroom.*

VICKI. Oh, you're in a real
state!

ROGER. Come on, then.

VICKI. You can't even get
the door open.

Exeunt ROGER *and* VICKI
into the bedroom.

*The sound of a key in the
lock, and the front door
opens. On the doorstep
stands* PHILIP, *carrying
a cardboard box. He is in
his forties, with a deep
suntan, and writes attractive
new plays with a charming
period atmosphere.*

BELINDA *enters from the
dressing-rooms, holding
the bottle of whisky.*

PHILIP. . . . Yes, but this is
Mrs Clackett's afternoon
off.

She gives the whisky to
DOTTY, *and just makes
her entrance.*

Enter FLAVIA. *She is in
her thirties, the perfect*

Enter SELSDON *from the dressing-rooms.*

He asks DOTTY *for the whisky.*

But she is distracted by GARRY, *who tells her that he will no longer tolerate these furtive meetings with* FREDERICK.

companion piece to the above.

We've got the place entirely to ourselves.

PHILIP *brings in a flight bag and closes the door.*

FLAVIA. Look at it!

PHILIP. Do you like it?

FLAVIA. I can't believe it!

PHILIP. The perfect place for an assignation.

FLAVIA. Home.

PHILIP. Home.

FLAVIA. Our little secret hideaway.

PHILIP. The last place on earth anyone will look for us.

FLAVIA. It's rather funny, creeping in like this. I wonder if Mrs Clackett's aired the beds.

PHILIP. Darling!

FLAVIA. Well, why not? No children. No friends dropping in. We're absolutely on our own.

SELSDON *tries urgently to take the whisky off them as they quarrel.*

GARRY *and* DOTTY *both turn on him in fury.*

GARRY *pleads with* DOTTY—*kneels—weeps —hangs on to her plate of sardines.*

PHILIP. True. (*Picks up the bag and box and ushers* FLAVIA *towards the stairs.*) There is something to be said for being a tax exile.

FLAVIA. Leave those!

He drops the bag and box and kisses her. She flees upstairs, laughing, and he after her.

PHILIP. Sh!

DOTTY *breaks away from* GARRY. SELSDON *points out that she is still holding the whisky.* GARRY *takes it off her as she makes her entrance.*

FLAVIA. What?

PHILIP. Inland Revenue may hear us!

They creep to the bedroom door.
Enter MRS CLACKETT *from the service quarters carrying a fresh plate of sardines.*

SELSDON *tries to get the whisky off* GARRY, *but* GARRY *turns to ascend the platform for his entrance.*

MRS CLACKETT (*to herself*): What I did with that first lot of sardines I shall never know.

She puts the sardines on the telephone table and sits on the sofa.

He looks round for something to do with the whisky, and gives it to BROOKE.

PHILIP *and* FLAVIA (*looking down from the gallery*): Mrs Clackett!

MRS CLACKETT *jumps up.*

BROOKE *peers at it, no idea what she's supposed to do with it.*
She asks SELSDON, *who wags a reproving finger at her for possessing such a dangerous substance, and takes it from her.*

MRS CLACKETT. Oh, you give me a turn! My heart jumped right out of my boots!

PHILIP. So did mine!

FLAVIA. We thought you'd gone!

He hides it.

Then he demonstrates to BROOKE *pulling a chain, and points at himself.*

BROOKE, *undressing for her next entrance, peers uncomprehendingly.*

Exit SELSDON *to the dressing-rooms with the whiskey.*

MRS CLACKETT. I thought you was in Spain!

PHILIP. We are! We are!

FLAVIA. You haven't seen us!

PHILIP. We're not here!

MRS CLACKETT. You'll want your things, look. (*Indicates the bag and box.*)

PHILIP. Oh. Yes. Thanks.

PHILIP *comes downstairs, and picks up the bag and box.*

MRS CLACKETT (*to* FLAVIA): Oh, and that bed hasn't been aired, love.

FLAVIA. I'll get a hot water bottle.

BELINDA *makes her exit.* BROOKE *tells* BELINDA *that* SELSDON *has been drinking.*

Exit FLAVIA *into the mezzanine bathroom.*

MRS CLACKETT. I've put all your letters in the study, dear.

PHILIP. Oh my God. Where are they?

MRS CLACKETT. I've put them all in the little pigeonhouse.

PHILIP. In the pigeonhouse?

MRS CLACKETT. In the little pigeonhouse in your desk, love.

GARRY, *still on the platform, tries to see what*

Exeunt MRS CLACKETT

DOTTY *and* FREDERICK
*are doing, but is fetched
back by* BROOKE *for his
entrance.*

DOTTY *sees* GARRY
*watching them, and
explains to* FREDERICK
that GARRY *now thinks
that* FREDERICK *is her
lover.
. . . By this time* BROOKE
has to make her entrance.

and PHILIP *into the study.*
PHILIP *is still holding the
bag and box.*
Enter ROGER *from the
bedroom, still dressed,
tying his tie.*

ROGER. Yes, but I could
hear voices!

Enter VICKI *from the
bedroom in her underwear.*

VICKI. Voices? What sort of
voices?

ROGER. People's voices.

VICKI (*looks over the
bannisters*): Oh, look, she's
opened our sardines.

She moves to go downstairs.
ROGER *grabs her.*

ROGER. Come back!

VICKI. What?

ROGER. I'll fetch them! You
can't go downstairs like
that.

VICKI. Why not?

BELINDA *urgently passes
on the demonstration of
elbow-raising to* DOTTY.
*But by the time she takes
it in, it's time for her
entrance.*

ROGER. Mrs Crackett.

VICKI. Mrs Crackett?

ROGER. She's irreplaceable.

Enter MRS CLACKETT
*from the study. She is
carrying the first plate of
sardines.*

MRS CLACKETT (*to herself*):
Sardines here. Sardines
there. It's like a Sunday
school outing.

BROOKE *makes her exit.*
and BELINDA *runs up to*
the platform to ask her
where SELSDON *is.*

ROGER *pushes* VICKI
through the first available
door, which happens to be
the linen cupboard.

Oh, you're still poking
around, are you?

BROOKE *points in the*
direction of the dressing-
rooms.

ROGER. Yes, still poking—
well, still around.

MRS CLACKETT. In the airing-
cupboard, were you?

ROGER. No, no. (*The linen*
cupboard door begins to
open. He slams it shut.)
Well, just checking the
sheets and pillow-cases.
Going through the inventory.

He starts downstairs.

Enter TIM *from the*
dressing-rooms with a
second, smaller, bunch of
flowers.

ROGER. Mrs Blackett . . .

MRS CLACKETT. Clackett,
dear, Clackett.

Exit BELINDA *to the*
dressing-rooms in haste.

She puts down the sardines
beside the other sardines.

TIM *asks* FREDERICK
where she is going.

ROGER. Mrs Clackett. Is
there anyone else in the
house, Mrs Clackett?

FREDERICK *demonstrates*
raising the elbow.
Enter BELINDA *from the*
dressing-rooms.
She demonstrates that
SELSDON *has locked him-*
self in somewhere.

MRS CLACKETT. I haven't
seen no one, dear.

ROGER. I thought I heard
voices.

MRS CLACKETT. Voices?
There's no voices here, love.

ROGER. I must have imagined
it.

PHILIP *says his line.*

PHILIP (*off*): Oh my God!

TIM *hands* BELINDA *the
flowers, and dashes out to
the dressing-rooms.*

ROGER, *with his back to
her, picks up both plates
of sardines.*

ROGER. I beg your pardon?

*She gives the flowers to
FREDERICK and fetches
the fireman's axe from the
fire point.*

MRS CLACKETT (*mimics
PHILIP*): Oh my God!

ROGER. Why, what is it?

*She is going to rush off to
the dressing-rooms with it
when* POPPY
*reminds her that she has
an entrance coming up.*
BELINDA *runs up on to
the platform, finds she is
still holding the axe, and
gives it to* BROOKE.

MRS CLACKETT. Oh my
God, the study door's
open.

She crosses and closes it.
ROGER *looks out of the
window.*

ROGER. There's another car
outside! That's not Mr
Hackham's, is it? Or
Mr Dudley's?

*But before she can explain
what to do with it,*
BELINDA *has to make her
entrance.*

Exit ROGER *through the
front door, holding both
plates of sardines.*

GARRY *advances threaten-
ingly upon* FREDERICK
*and gazes suspiciously at
the flowers he is holding.*
FREDERICK *has to hand
GARRY the flowers in
order to make his entrance.*

Enter FLAVIA *from the
mezzanine bathroom,
carrying a hot water bottle.
She sees the linen cupboard
door open as she passes,
pushes it shut, and turns
the key.*

BROOKE *comes down*

FLAVIA. Nothing but flapping
doors in this house.

*from the platform and
asks* GARRY *what she is
supposed to do with the
axe.* GARRY *takes it
thoughtfully, and puts the
flowers into her hands. He
looks at the axe, then
whirls it up over his head
to wait for* FREDERICK'S
exit.

BELINDA *comes down
from the platform to go
off after* SELSDON. *She
sees* GARRY *and is
horrified. She quickly takes
the flowers from* BROOKE
and sends her off to fetch
SELSDON.
BELINDA *tries to get the
axe away from* GARRY.
He holds it behind his back.
BELINDA, *still holding
the flowers, puts her arms
round* GARRY, *trying to
reach the axe.*

DOTTY *appears just in
time to see* BELINDA
with her arms round
GARRY.

POPPY *urges* BELINDA
upstairs.

BELINDA *flees up on to
the platform to make her
entrance. She makes one
desperate effort to grab
the dress, then enters still
carrying the flowers instead.*

Exit FLAVIA *into the
bedroom.
Enter from the study*
PHILIP, *holding a tax
demand and its envelope.*

PHILIP. '. . . final notice . . .
steps will be taken . . .
distraint . . . proceedings
in court . . .'

MRS CLACKETT. Oh yes,
and that reminds me, a
gentleman come about the
house.

PHILIP. Don't tell me. I'm not
here.

MRS CLACKETT. So I'll
just sit down and turn on
the . . . sardines, I've
forgotten the sardines! I
don't know—if it wasn't
fixed to my shoulders I'd
forget what day it was.

Exit MRS CLACKETT *to
the service quarters.*

PHILIP. I didn't get this! I'm
not here. I'm in Spain. But
if I didn't get it I didn't
open it.

Enter FLAVIA *from the
bedroom. She is holding
the dress that* VICKI
arrived in.

BELINDA, *on stage, has to vary the line.*

DOTTY *launches herself upon* GARRY. *He produces the axe in explanation.* DOTTY *snatches it, and raises it to hit* GARRY.

FREDERICK *appears, and snatches the axe from* DOTTY, *in the nick of time. He innocently gives it to* GARRY, *who raises it to hit* FREDERICK. DOTTY *snatches it from* GARRY, *and raises it to hit him.* BELINDA *appears and snatches the axe from* DOTTY, *as* GARRY *makes his entrance.* Enter TIM *from the dressing-rooms. He grabs the axe from* BELINDA *and returns to the dressing-rooms.*

BELINDA *is going to follow him, but then*

FLAVIA. Darling, I never had a dress, or rather bunch of flowers like this, did I?

PHILIP (*abstracted*): Didn't you?

FLAVIA. I shouldn't buy anything as tarty as this . . . Oh, it's not something you gave me, is it?

PHILIP. I should never have touched it.

FLAVIA. No, it's lovely.

PHILIP. Stick it down. Put it back. Never saw it.

Exit PHILIP *into study.*

FLAVIA. Well, I'll put it in the attic, with all the other things you gave me that are too precious to wear.

Exit FLAVIA *along the upstairs corridor.*

Enter ROGER *through the front door, still carrying both plates of sardines.*

ROGER. All right, all right . . . Now the study door's open again! What's going on?

He puts the sardines down— one plate on the telephone table, where it was before, one near the front door— and goes towards the study, realises that there is no knocking because BROOKE *is still off.*

but stops at the sound of urgent knocking overhead. Knocking!

GARRY, *on stage repeats the cue.*

Knocking . . . ! Knocking? Upstairs!

BELINDA *realises what's wrong, and knocks on the set with a prop.*

Runs upstairs. Knocking. Oh my God, there's something in the airing cupboard!

Only BROOKE *doesn't make her entrance, because she is still off.*

Unlocks it and opens it. Enter VICKI.

ROGER. Oh, it's you.

GARRY *comes through the linen cupboard door to look for* BROOKE.

GARRY *improvises.*

Is it you . . . ? I mean, you know, hidden under all the sheets and towels in here . I can't just stand here and, you know, indefinitely . . .

BELINDA *tells* POPPY *to read in* BROOKE's *part from the book. Then she hands the flowers to* FREDERICK *and runs off to the dressing-rooms, still holding the axe.*

POPPY (*reads*): Of course it's me! You put me in here! In the dark! With all black sheets and things!

ROGER. But, darling, why did you lock the door?

POPPY. Why did *I* lock the door? Why did *you* lock the door!

ROGER. *I* didn't lock the door!

Enter LLOYD *through the
pass door. He demands
silently to know what's
going on.* FREDERICK
*tries to explain,
while* POPPY *and* GARRY
continue to play the scene.

POPPY. *Someone* locked the
door!

ROGER. Anyway, we can't
stand here like this.

FREDERICK *hands*
LLOYD *the flowers to
make ready for his
entrance.* LLOYD *hurriedly
soothes* DOTTY.

POPPY. Like what?

ROGER. In your underwear.

POPPY. OK, I'll take it off.

ROGER. In here, in here!

Exit ROGER *into the
bedroom.
Enter* PHILIP *from the
study, holding the tax
demand, the envelope, and
a tube of glue.*

LLOYD *shoves the flowers
into* DOTTY's *hands to get
rid of them, and tears*
POPPY's *skirt off, so that
she can go on for* BROOKE.

PHILIP. Darling, this glue.
It's not that special quick-
drying sort, is it, that you
can never get unstuck . . .
Oh, Mrs Clackett's made us
some sardines.

Enter BELINDA *from the
dressing-rooms, with*
BROOKE. BROOKE *peers
at the undressing of*
POPPY.

Exit PHILIP *into the study
with the tax demand,
envelope, glue, and the
plate of sardines from the
telephone table.
Enter* ROGER *from the*

LLOYD *abandons* POPPY,
and urges BROOKE *up the
stairs for her next scene,
for which she is now late.*

GARRY *comes back through
the bedroom door to look
for* BROOKE.
He improvises.

*bedroom, holding the hot
water bottle. He looks up
and down the landing.*

ROGER. A hot water bottle!
I didn't put it there!

I didn't put this hot water
bottle, I mean, you know,
I'm standing out there,
with the hot water bottle
in my hands . . .

BROOKE *makes her
entrance through the linen
cupboard door, and starts
playing the previous scene
that she missed.*

DOTTY *asks* LLOYD *if
the flowers are really for
her. He pushes them back
to her absently, concerned
about* BROOKE *onstage.*
DOTTY *is very touched.
She gives* LLOYD *a grateful
kiss, just as* GARRY
appears to see it.

VICKI. Of course it's me! You
put me in here! In the dark!
With all black sheets and
things!

ROGER. Someone in the
bathroom, filling hot water
bottles . . . What?

Exit ROGER *into the
mezzanine bathroom.*

VICKI. But, darling, why did
you lock the door?

GARRY *moves closer to
see, and cuts three pages
of script.*
*He panics, unable for a
moment to think where he
is, then enters through the
airing-cupboard instead of
the bedroom.*
*Everyone backstage
panics: 'Where are we?'*

ROGER. Don't panic! Don't
panic!

Enter ROGER, *and goes
downstairs.*

There's some perfectly
rational explanation for all
this. I'll fetch Mrs Splotchett

POPPY *desperately turns over the pages of the book to find the new place, while people look over her shoulder.*

Enter TIM *from the dressing-rooms, leading a bewildered* SELSDON, *who is holding his trousers up.* TIM *is holding the axe and the whiskey. He hands the whiskey to* FREDERICK. FREDERICK *roars with surprise.*

FREDERICK *hastily conceals the whisky under the chairs and makes his entrance.*

TIM *gives the axe to* LLOYD *and takes the flowers from* DOTTY, *who snatches them right back, leaving* TIM *with only one. He hands this to* LLOYD, *who hands it to* BROOKE. *She peers at it as it keels sadly over.* LLOYD *gives money to* TIM *who exits wearily to the dressing-rooms.*

and she'll tell us what's happening. You wait here . . You can't stand here looking like that . . . You wait in the study . . . Study, study, study!

Exit ROGER *into the service quarters.*

VICKI *opens the study door. There is a roar of exasperation from* PHILIP, *off. She turns and flees.*

VICKI. Roger! There's something in there! Where are you?

There is another cry from PHILIP, *off. Exit* VICKI *blindly through the front door.*
Enter PHILIP *from the study. He is holding the tax demand in his right hand, and one of the plates of sardines in his left.*

PHILIP. Darling, I know this is going to sound silly, but . . .

He struggles to get the tax demand unstuck from his fingers, encumbered by the plate of sardines.

Enter FLAVIA *along the upstairs corridor, carrying various pieces of bric-a-brac*

FLAVIA. Darling, if we're not
going to bed I'm going to
clear out the attic.

PHILIP. Darling, I can't come
to bed! I'm glued to a tax
demand!

FLAVIA. Darling, why don't
you put the sardines down?

SELSDON is explaining to
everyone where he was, by
a show of pulling a chain.
This demonstration causes
his trousers to fall down.

PHILIP *puts the plate of*
sardines down on the table.
But when he takes his hand
away the sardines come
with it.

PHILIP. Darling, I'm stuck to
the sardines!

FLAVIA. Darling, don't play
the fool. Get that bottle
marked poison in the
downstairs loo. That eats
through anything.

Exit FLAVIA along the
upstairs corridor.

SELSDON stoops to
retrieve his fallen trousers,
and sees the whisky that
FREDERICK concealed
beneath the chairs. He
picks it up, and LLOYD
snatches it out of his hand
and gives it to DOTTY.

PHILIP (*flaps the tax demand*):
I've heard of people getting
stuck with a problem, but
this is ridiculous.

Exit PHILIP into the
downstairs bathroom.

FREDERICK *repeats the*
cue, and slams the door
again.

PHILIP. But this is ridiculous.

They all suddenly realise
that this is SELSDON's
cue. They rush him to the
window. He raises his arms

Exit PHILIP into the
downstairs bathroom.

to open the window and his trousers fall down. They bundle him on as best they can.

A pane of glass shatters in the mullioned window, and an arm comes through and releases the catch. The window opens, and through it appears an elderly BURGLAR. *He has great character, but is in need of extensive repair and modernisation.*

BURGLAR. No bars, no burglar alarm. They ought to be prosecuted for incitement.

He climbs in.

No, but sometimes it makes me want to sit down and weep. When I think I used to do banks! When I remember I used to do bullion vaults! What am I doing now?—I'm breaking into paper bags!

Pours himself a drink.

I know they're all in Spain, 'cause the old turkey in the kitchen told me so. And I know *she's* out, 'cause I've just seen her come out of the front door in her swimming costume . . . Where is the front door . . . ?

GARRY *snatches the flowers from* DOTTY. *She snatches them back.*

LLOYD *parts them with the axe. He gently takes the flowers from* DOTTY *and hands them to* FREDERICK *while he gives the axe to* BELINDA.
BELINDA *uses the axe to keep* DOTTY *and* GARRY *apart.* FREDERICK *hands the flowers to* POPPY, *explaining that they are from* LLOYD. POPPY, *touched, takes this as the cue to come down and say what she has to say to* LLOYD. BROOKE *myopically compares her miserable flower with* POPPY*'s full bunch.*

LLOYD, *pursued by*
POPPY, *and takes a*
fortifying swig of whisky.
POPPY *watches him. So*
does SELSDON, *as he*
looks through the front
door. He dries in
amazement.

Peers short-sightedly, then
opens the front door ready
for his departure.

SELSDON. Yes? Yes? Line?
Prompt?

POPPY *runs back with the*
flowers to the corner to
give him his prompt.

POPPY. Right, get the van
loaded up.

SELSDON. What?

OMNES (*shout*): Get the van
loaded up!

SELSDON *runs back on.*
BROOKE *throws her single*
flower back at LLOYD *and*
goes off to the dressing-
rooms, hurt.

Right, get the van loaded
up. No rush. I've only got
all flaming afternoon!
Right, what are they
offering? (*Peers at the*
television.) One microwave
oven.

FREDERICK, *realising he*
has been tactless, insists
to LLOYD *that he will go*
after her.

Unplugs it and puts it on
the sofa.

What? Fifty quid? Hardly
worth lifting it.

LLOYD *demonstrates*
the danger of tears washing
away her lenses.

Picks up his drink and
inspects the paintings and
ornaments.

Junk . . . Junk . . . If you
insist . . .

BELINDA, *with the axe,*
escorts DOTTY *and*
GARRY *to make their*
entrance.

BELINDA *takes the*
whisky from LLOYD *and*
holds it up to see how
much has been drunk.
She expresses shock to
SELSDON, *who takes the*
whisky from her, and wags
his finger reproachfully
at LLOYD.

LLOYD *tries to get the*
bottle away from him.

SELSDON, *shocked at this*
open craving, keeps the
bottle out of his reach.

Enter TIM *with a third, very*
small, bunch of flowers. He
gives them to LLOYD, *very*
insistent that they are put
into his hands directly.

Pockets some small item.

Where's his desk? No, the'
all say the same thing—it':
hard to adjust to retiremen

Exit BURGLAR *into the*
study, holding his drink.

Enter ROGER *from the*
service quarters, followed
by MRS CLACKETT, *who*
is holding another plate
of sardines.

ROGER. . . . And the
prospective tenant natural!
wishes to know if there is
any previous history of
paranormal phenomena.

MRS CLACKETT. Oh, yes,
dear, it's all nice and
paranormal.

ROGER. I mean, has anything
ever dematerialised before
Has anything ever flown
about?

MRS CLACKETT *puts the*
sardines down on the
telephone table, moves the
television set back, plugs it
in, and closes the front doc

MRS CLACKETT. Flown
about? No, the things mov(
themselves on their own
two feet, just like they do
in any house.

ROGER. I'll tell the prospective
tenant. She is inspecting th(
study.

He opens the study door
and then closes it again.

There's a man in there!

MRS CLACKETT. No, no,
there's no one in the house,
love.

LLOYD *hands the flowers*
to BELINDA *while he*
deals with SELSDON.
SELSDON *conceals the*
whiskey in a fire
bucket while LLOYD
is distracted by
BELINDA.

SELSDON *demonstrates*
that his hands are empty.
LLOYD *searches him.*

ROGER (*opens the study*
door): Look! Look! He's
. . . searching for something.

MRS CLACKETT (*glances*
briefly): I can't see no one.

ROGER. You can't see him?
But this is extraordinary!
And where is my
prospective tenant? I left
her in there! She's gone!
My prospective tenant has
disappeared!

She hands the axe to TIM
and gives LLOYD *a grateful*
kiss.
Enter FREDERICK *from*
the dressing-rooms, bring-
ing BROOKE *back.*
She peers at the spectacle
of BELINDA, *with*
flowers, kissing LLOYD.

He closes the study door,
and looks round the living
room. He sees the sardines
on the telephone table.

Oh my God.

MRS CLACKETT. Now what?

ROGER. There!

MRS CLACKETT. Where?

ROGER. The sardines!

MRS CLACKETT. Oh, the
sardines.

TIM, *seeing this, hands the*
axe to FREDERICK, *and*
wearily holds out his hand
for money.
LLOYD *wearily gives him*
his last small change.

Exit TIM *to the dressing-*

rooms. BELINDA *suddenly
realises that her flowers
are attracting jealous
attention, and puts them
on* POPPY'*s table with the
other flowers.*

BROOKE *turns to go back
to the dressing-rooms,
upset again.*
LLOYD *stops her, and
looks round for some
token of his affection to
give her instead of the
flowers.*

FREDERICK, *tidily
putting the axe back on
the firepoint, finds the
whisky and holds it aloft—
another bottle!*

SELSDON *takes the bottle
from* FREDERICK, *but*
LLOYD *takes it from*
SELSDON *in time for*
SELSDON *to make his
entrance.*
LLOYD *gives the whisky
to* BROOKE, *but* FREDERICK
*takes it out of his
hands to hide it.*

LLOYD *takes it back.*
FREDERICK *takes it away
again.*

ROGER. You can see the
sardines, can you?

MRS CLACKETT. I can see
the sardines.

ROGER *touches them
cautiously, then picks up
the plate.*

I can see the way they're
going, too.

ROGER. I'm not letting these
sardines out of my hand.
But where is my prospective
tenant?

*He goes upstairs, holding
the sardines.*

MRS CLACKETT. I can see
I'm going to be opening
sardines all night, in and
out of here like the cuckoo
on a clock.

Exit MRS CLACKETT
into the service quarters.

ROGER. Vicki! Vicki!

Exit ROGER *into the
mezzanine bathroom.
Enter* BURGLAR *from the
study, carrying an armful
of silver cups, etc.*

BURGLAR. He said, 'Charles,'
he said. 'You're seventy
years old. It's time to hang
up the sawn-off shotgun.
It's time to let a younger
man take over the ammonia
bottle.

LLOYD *retrieves it.*
FREDERICK *takes it and*
hides it on the platform.

Dumps the silverware on
the sofa, and exits into the
study.
Enter ROGER *from*
mezzanine bathroom.

ROGER. Where's she gone?
She hasn't gone back in
the bedroom?

GARRY *makes his exit*

Exit ROGER *into the*
bedroom.
Enter BURGLAR *from*
the study, carrying
PHILIP's *box and bag.*
He empties out the contents
of the box behind the sofa,
and loads the silverware
into it.

BURGLAR. I said, 'I may
be seventy, but I've still
got all my wits about me.'
He didn't have any answer
to that.

He leans down and tips the
plate of sardines he is
carrying over DOTTY's
head, then makes his
entrance.

Enter ROGER *from the*
bedroom, still holding the
sardines.

ROGER (*calls*): Vicki! Vicki!

GARRY *makes his exit,*
picks up the whisky, and
takes a swig.

Exit ROGER *into the*
linen cupboard.

While his head is back,
DOTTY *ties his shoelaces*
together.

BURGLAR. Or if he did, *I*
didn't hear it.

Exit BURGLAR *into study,*
not having seen or heard
ROGER.
Enter PHILIP *from the*

downstairs bathroom. His right hand is still stuck to the tax demand, his left to the plate of sardines.

PHILIP. Darling, this stuff in the bottle. It *doesn't* eat through glue . . . It just eats through *trousers!* Darling, if it eats through trousers, you don't think it goes on and eats through . . . Listen, darling, I think I'd better get these trousers off! (*He begins to do so, as best he can.*) Darling, quick, this is an emergency! Have we got any stuff that stops the stuff that stops the stuff? I mean, if it eats through absolutely anything . . . Darling, I think I can feel it! I think it's eating through . . . absolutely everything!

LLOYD *tries to warn* GARRY. GARRY *brushes him aside because he has an entrance coming up.*

GARRY *puts the whisky down and makes his entrance, falling over his feet.*

Enter ROGER *from the linen cupboard, still holding the sardines.*

ROGER. There's something evil in this house.

PHILIP *pulls up his trousers.*

PHILIP (*aside*): The Inland Revenue!

DOTTY *demonstrates to* BELINDA *and* LLOYD *what she did.*
They all three try to see what's happening on stage.

ROGER (*frightened*): He's back!

SELSDON *finds the bottle on the platform—yet another bottle!*

PHILIP. No!

ROGER. No?

LLOYD *takes it away from him mechanically.*

LLOYD, DOTTY *and* BELINDA *all take swigs from it in turn, absent-mindedly, as they follow events on stage.*

SELSDON *just misses it each time as they pass it absently from hand to hand.*

DOTTY *holds up her hands for silence, and they all wait for the crash.*

The sounds of GARRY *falling downstairs on stage, which even* SELSDON *can hear.*

PHILIP. I'm not here.

ROGER. Oh my God.

PHILIP. I'm abroad.

ROGER. He's walking abroad.

PHILIP. I must go.

ROGER. Stay!

PHILIP. I'm not staying.

ROGER. Speak!

PHILIP. Only in the presence of my lawyer.

ROGER. Only in the . . . ? Hold on. Hold on. You're just an intruder, an ordinary intruder!

PHILIP. Well, nice to meet you.

Waves goodbye with his right hand, then sees the tax demand on it, and hurriedly puts it away behind his back.

I mean, have a sardine.

Offers the sardines on his left hand. His trousers, unsupported, fall down.

ROGER. No, you're not! You're a sex criminal! I'm going to come downstairs and sort you out.

ROGER *comes downstairs.*

PHILIP. Oh, you've got some sardines. Well, if there's nothing I can offer you . . .

No response on stage from
GARRY. *They listen, and*
as they listen their
laughter dies away.
FREDERICK, *on stage,*
improvises a line.   Are you all right?
No reply.
BELINDA *turns to* DOTTY
in horror: You've killed
him! BELINDA *opens*
the study door to go to
GARRY. LLOYD *restrains*
her.
DOTTY *throws her arms*
round the first person to
hand, who happens to be
BROOKE, *and cries silently*
in an agony of remorse: I've
killed him!
BROOKE *looks amazed,*
then claps her hands to
her eyes.

At the sound of GARRY's   ROGER (*into the phone*):
voice, they all relax.   Police!

LLOYD *takes another swig*   PHILIP. . . . . I think I'll be
of whisky.   running along.

                                   Runs, his trousers still
                                   round his ankles.
FREDERICK *makes his*   *Exit through front door.*
exit, trousers round his
ankles, handkerchief   ROGER. Come back . . . !
pressed to his nose.   (*Into the phone:*) Hello—
BELINDA *hugs him.* DOTTY   police! Someone has
tears him away from her   broken into my house! Or
and hugs him. BELINDA   rather someone has broken
tears him back again.   into someone's house . . .
DOTTY *snatches the whiskey*   Yes, a sex criminal! And a
bottle from LLOYD *to hit*   young woman is missing!

BELINDA, *but she hits* BROOKE
instead. BROOKE *loses her
lenses.*
*Everyone is now occupied
by this next problem.*
GARRY *repeats the cue.*
BROOKE *is guided to the
window for her entrance.*

Enter BROOKE *through
the window.*

VICKI. It's in the garden now,
and it's a man!

ROGER (*into the phone*):
Sorry—the young woman
has reappeared. (*Hand over
phone.*) Are you all right?

VICKI. No, he almost saw me!

ROGER (*into the phone*): He
almost saw her . . . No, but
he's a burglar as well! He's
taken our things!

VICKI (*finds* PHILIP's *bags*):
The things are here.

ROGER (*into the phone*): The
things have come back. So
we're just missing a plate of
sardines.

SELSDON *suggests to*
DOTTY *that the lenses may
be in her clothes.*

VICKI (*finds the sardines left
near the front door by*
ROGER): Here are the
sardines.

ROGER (*into the phone*):
And we've found the
sardines.

VICKI. This is the police? You
want the police here—in
my underwear?

ROGER (*into the phone*): So
what am I saying? I'm
saying, let's say no more
about it. (*Puts the phone
down.*) I thought something
terrible had happened to
you!

VICKI. It has! I know him!

ROGER. You know him?

POPPY *asks* LLOYD *if
this is a good moment for
their talk.
He waves her away.*

VICKI. He's dealt with by
our office!

ROGER. He's just an ordinary
sex criminal!

VICKI. Yes, but he mustn't
see me like this! You have
to keep up certain standards
if you work for Inland
Revenue!

SELSDON *searches*
DOTTY's *clothes. She
can't understand what
he's after.*

ROGER. Well, put something
on!

VICKI. I haven't got anything!

ROGER. There must be
something in the bathroom!

*He picks up the box
and bag and leads the way
upstairs towards the
mezzanine bathroom.*

Bring the sardines!

GARRY *comes raging off,
his shoes still tied together.
He gazes in amazement at
the sight of* DOTTY *and*
SELSDON *below.* GARRY
repeats the cue.

Exeunt ROGER *and* VICKI
*into the mezzanine
bathroom.*

LLOYD *rushes* SELSDON
on.

GARRY *starts down the*
stairs to sort people out,
but the state of his shoes
prevents his getting more
than a step or two before
he has to return to make
his entrance.

FREDERICK *takes over*
the search in DOTTY's
clothes.

GARRY, *gazing furiously*
down at FREDERICK *and*
DOTTY, *moves to attack*
FREDERICK.

Enter the BURGLAR
from the study, carrying
a tape-recorder.

BURGLAR. 'What?' I said.
'When have I ever needed
to run off in the middle of
a job to have a Jimmy
Riddle?'

Puts the tape-recorder
down by the front door.

BURGLAR. 'Except when
some stupid berk goes and
starts talking about it . . . ?'

Oh, my Gawd! Where is it?

Enter ROGER *from the*
mezzanine bathroom,
carrying the box and bags.

ROGER. Just stay in there,
and don't come out till
you've got dressed.

Enter VICKI *from the*
mezzanine bathroom,
holding up a very short
off-the-shoulder white
nightdress.

Exit ROGER *into the*
bedroom.

VICKI. But I can't go around
in front of our taxpayers
wearing *this!*

Exit VICKI *into the*
bedroom.

BURGLAR. I knew I shouldn't
have brought the subject
up.

But GARRY *is still
hobbled, and* FREDERICK
*has to make
his entrance.*

GARRY *tries to get*
BROOKE *to untie him. But
she has to make her
entrance.*

TIM *enters from the
dressing rooms, carrying
a cactus, which he gives
to* LLOYD.
GARRY *cries out at the
sight of* LLOYD *peering
into* DOTTY'S *clothing.*
LLOYD *hands the cactus to*
DOTTY, *who absently
hands it to* GARRY. LLOYD
bends over DOTTY'S *clothes
again, and* GARRY *rams
the cactus up against*
LLOYD'S *bottom. Then*
GARRY *hobbles back
upstairs, still holding the
cactus.* LLOYD *tries to
pursue him, but is stopped
by the pain.*
GARRY *puts the cactus
down on the platform. He
takes the ends of the bedsheets that are hanging up
outside the bedroom door,
waiting for* FREDERICK
and BROOKE, *and ties
them together.*

Exit BURGLAR *into the
open door of the mezzanine
bathroom.*
Enter PHILIP *through the
front door.*

PHILIP. Darling! Help! Where
are you?

Enter VICKI *from the
bedroom, holding the
nightdress, followed by*
ROGER.
Exit PHILIP *hurriedly
into the downstairs bath-
room.*

ROGER. Just put it on! It's a
start, at any rate! I'll find
a bottom—I'll find a top—
I'll find something.

Exit ROGER *into the
bedroom.*
Exit VICKI *into the
mezzanine bathroom.*
Enter VICKI *from the
mezzanine bathroom.*

VICKI. Someone in there! It's
him!

Exit VICKI *hurriedly into
the downstairs bathroom.*
Enter FLAVIA *along
upstairs corridor, carrying
an old biscuit tin.*

FLAVIA. Oh, darling, I'm
finding such lovely things!

VICKI *screams off.*

Do you remember this old
biscuit tin . . .

Enter VICKI *from the downstairs bathroom. She stops at the sight of* FLAVIA.

. . . you gave me on the very first anniversary of our . . . ? Who are you?

VICKI. Oh my God, it's his wife and dependents!

She puts her hands over her face.

Enter PHILIP *from the downstairs bathroom, still with his hands encumbered, holding the nightdress now as well, and keeping his trousers up with his elbows.*

PHILIP. I've taken your dress off you!

FLAVIA *gasps.* PHILIP *looks up at the gallery and sees her.*

PHILIP (*to* FLAVIA): Where have you been? I've been going mad! Look at the state I'm in!

He holds up his hands to show FLAVIA *the state he is in, and his trousers fall down.*
The biscuit tin slips from FLAVIA's *horrified hands, and crashes on the floor of the living room below.* PHILIP *hurries towards*

*the stairs, trousers around
his ankles, hands extended
in supplication.*

BROOKE *makes her exit,
and* GARRY *points out the*

VICKI *flees before him and
takes refuge in the linen
cupboard.*

PHILIP. Darling, I was just
trying to explain to her
about Inland Revenue being
after us, and my fingers
got stuck!

*cactus as he passes her
on the way to make his
entrance.*
BROOKE *comes down
from the platform holding
the cactus.* DOTTY *pulls
a cactus needle out of*
LLOYD's *bottom.*

Exit FLAVIA, *with a cry
of pain, along the upstairs
corridor.*
Enter ROGER *from the
bedroom, directly in*
PHILIP's *path.* PHILIP
*holds up the nightdress
in front of his face.*

ROGER. Don't keep waving
that thing in my face! I'm
trying to find something!
I'll look in the other rooms.

Exit ROGER *along
upstairs corridor.*
PHILIP *turns to go back
downstairs. The mezzanine
lavatory flushes. He stops.
Enter the* BURGLAR *from
the mezzanine bathroom,
holding two gold taps.*

BROOKE *stands gazing
in amazement as* LLOYD
*lowers his trousers and
bends over, while* DOTTY
*pulls needles out of his
bottom.*
BELINDA *watches the
scene from the platform.
So does* GARRY.
TIM *warns* LLOYD *that*
GARRY *is hobbling
downstairs again.*

BURGLAR. One pair gold
taps, anyway . . .

He stops at the sight of
PHILIP.

LLOYD *quickly pulls up his trousers.*
TIM *takes the cactus from* BROOKE *before* GARRY *can get it and use it again.*

GARRY *has to turn back and go up to the platform again to make his entrance.*

LLOYD *lowers his trousers again for* DOTTY *to resume operations.*

GARRY *makes his exit, and* LLOYD *hurriedly decides that he needs no further attention.*

BURGLAR. Oh, my Gawd!

PHILIP. Who are you?

BURGLAR. Me? Fixing the taps.

PHILIP. Tax? Income tax?

BURGLAR. That's right, governor. In come the new taps—out go the old taps.

Exit BURGLAR *into the mezzanine bathroom.*

PHILIP. Tax-inspectors everywhere!

ROGER (*off*): Oh my God!

PHILIP. The other one!

Exit PHILIP *into the bedroom, holding the nightdress in front of his face.*
Enter ROGER *along the upstairs corridor.*

ROGER. Tin boxes flying about! There *is* something funny going on here! Are you dressed yet?

Exit ROGER *into mezzanine bathroom.*
Enter PHILIP *from the bedroom, trying to pull the nightdress off his head.*

PHILIP. Darling! I've got it stuck to my head now!

Enter ROGER *from the mezzanine bathroom.*

FREDERICK *makes his*
exit and picks up the
bedsheets which are waiting
for him and BROOKE *to*
put on. He flaps them at
BROOKE *from the plat-*
form to remind her about
her change.

BROOKE *peers at the*
flapping sheets, and turns
to go. But LLOYD *detains*
her while he takes the
cactus from TIM *and gives*
it to her, explaining that
it is a token of his
continuing affection. She
peers at it, and he takes
in the nature of the present
for the first time himself.
He turns in pained query
to TIM *who gestures*
that it was all the shop had
left—all the rest of their
stock is now on POPPY's
desk. FREDERICK *flaps*
the sheets in desperation.
BROOKE *runs up the*
steps with the cactus.

Exit PHILIP *into the*
bedroom.

ROGER. A man!

Enter the BURGLAR *from*
the mezzanine bathroom.

BURGLAR. Just doing the
taps, governor.

ROGER. Attacks? Not—
attacks on women?

BURGLAR. Try anything,
governor, but I'll do the
taps on the bath first.

Exit the BURGLAR *into*
the mezzanine bathroom.

ROGER. Sex criminals everywhere! Where is Vicki?
Vicki . . . ?

Exit ROGER *into*
downstairs bathroom.
Enter BURGLAR *from*
mezzanine bathroom,
heading for the front door.

BURGLAR. People everywhere!
I'm off. A tax on women?
I don't know, they'll put
a tax on anything these
days.

Enter ROGER *from the*
downstairs bathroom.
The BURGLAR *makes a*
U-turn and heads back
towards the mezzanine
bathroom.

ROGER. If I can't find her,
you're going to be in
trouble, you see.

SELSDON *makes his exit.*
BROOKE *pushes the cactus
into* SELSDON's *hands as
she passes.*
*There is a swirl of sheets
as* FREDERICK *attempts
to dress* BROOKE *in time
for her entrance. They
end up zipped together,
and attempting to enter
through separate doors.*
BELINDA, *upstairs for her
entrance, goes to try and
disentangle them.*
SELSDON, *standing
outside the mezzanine
bathroom, joins in. He is
still holding the cactus. He
and the cactus together
make things worse.*

FREDERICK *and* BROOKE
miss their entrance.
GARRY *seeing the situa-
tion, makes his entrance,
cursing that once again he
is the one who has to hold
the fort. He improvises.*

TIM *puts the sheet on, ready
to go on as* PHILIP's *double.*
LLOYD *makes him take it off
again and passes it up to*
FREDERICK *as an alternative
costume. But* FREDERICK
*has no time to put it on,
because he is dragged on*

BURGLAR. W.C.? I'll fix it.

Exit BURGLAR *into
mezzanine bathroom.*

ROGER. Vicki . . . ?

Exit ROGER *through
the front door.*

Enter ROGER *through the
front door.*

ROGER. No sheikh yet? I
thought he was coming at
four? I mean, it's nearly,
you know, four now . . .
Well, it's after three . . .
Because I've been standing
here for a good, you know,
it seems like forever . . .
What's the time now? It
must be getting on for, you
know . . . it must be getting
on for *five* . . .

*through the bedroom door
by* BROOKE.

Oh, you're here already,
hiding in the, anyway . . .
And this is your charming
wife? So you want to see
over the house now, do you,
Sheikh? Right. Well. Since
you're upstairs already . . .

ROGER *goes upstairs.*

Enter FLAVIA *along the
upstairs corridor, carrying
a vase.*

FLAVIA. Him and his floozie!
I'll break this over their
heads!

ROGER. . . . let's start
downstairs.

LLOYD *runs upstairs and
tries to recover* TIM's *sheet
from* FREDERICK.
FREDERICK, *onstage, keeps
trying to pass the sheet to*
LLOYD *through various doors.
But whichever door he tries,*
LLOYD *is always at the
wrong one.*

ROGER, PHILIP, *and* VICKI
go downstairs.

FLAVIA. Who are you? Who
are these creatures?

ROGER (*to* PHILIP *and*
VICKI): I'm sorry about
this. I don't know who she
is. No connection with the
house, I assure you.

Enter MRS CLACKETT
*from the service quarters,
with another plate of
sardines.* ROGER *advances
to introduce her.*

Whereas this good lady
with the sardines, on the
other hand . . .

MRS CLACKETT. No other hands, thank you, not in my sardines, 'cause this time I'm eating them.

ROGER ushers PHILIP and VICKI away from MRS CLACKETT towards the mezzanine bathroom.

He opens the door to the mezzanine bathroom.

But in here . . .

FLAVIA. *Arab* sheets?

Exit FLAVIA into the bedroom.
Enter the BURGLAR from the mezzanine bathroom.

ROGER. In here we have . . .

BURGLAR. Ballcocks, governor. Your ballcocks have gone.

LLOYD gives up. TIM, in burnous and dinner jacket, wants to know what he is supposed to wear. LLOYD improvises Arab robes for him by putting his raincoat on him back to front.

ROGER. Oh, we have him.

Enter FLAVIA from the bedroom.

FLAVIA. They're *Irish* sheets! Irish linen sheets off my own bed!

MRS CLACKETT. Oh, the thieving devils!

ROGER. In the *study*, however . . .

MRS CLACKETT. You give me that sheet, you devil!

*She seizes the nearest sheet,
and it comes away in her
hand to reveal* VICKI.
FLAVIA *comes downstairs
menacingly.*
Exit PHILIP *discreetly into
the study.*

FREDERICK *makes his
exit—with* BROOKE,
*since he is still all of
piece with her.*

SELSDON *improvises a
line.*

BURGLAR. It's my little girl!
So far as I could see before
she went.

BROOKE *gives her line off.*

VICKI. Dad!

FLAVIA *stops.*

TIM *makes his entrance.*

Enter PHILIP *from the
study in amazement.* (*He
is now played by a double.*)

BURGLAR. Our little Vicki,
that ran away from home,
I thought I'd never see
again!

FREDERICK *tries to disintangle
himself from the sheets.*
LLOYD *helps him to a
double-quick change.*
FREDERICK *turns around
just as* LLOYD *crams the
burnous onto his head, so
that it hangs over his face
instead of his neck.* LLOYD
crams the SHEIKH's *dark
glasses over the burnous,
just in time for* FREDERICK
*to stumble blindly on for
his entrance as the* SHEIKH.

PHILIP *collapses behind
the sofa, clutching at his
heart, unnoticed by the
others.*

LLOYD *picks up the*
whisky from wherever
TIM *left it. He takes a weary*
swig, and is just about to
sit down on the cactus,
when he springs up again
guiltily, because POPPY
is standing in front of him
reproachfully. She begins
to speak anxiously to him, at
first in a completely inaudible
whisper.

POPPY. Listen, I've got to
talk to you *now.* I'm sorry,
I know it's not a good
moment—it's never a good
moment. I keep trying
to phone you, but you're
never there. I know you're
in rehearsals all day, but
you're not there at night,
either, you're not there in
the morning—I don't
know *where* you are.

LLOYD *gestures that he*
can't hear, and offers her a
soothing sip of whisky. She
brushes it aside, becoming
more and more agitated.

POPPY (*voicing the words,*
which are still drowned
by the dialogue on stage):
No, no, no, I'm not going
to be put off, I'm going

FLAVIA (*threateningly*): So
where's my other sheet?

Enter through the front
door the most sought-after
of all properties on the
market today—a SHEIKH.
He is wearing Arab robes,
and bears a strong resem-
blance to PHILIP, *since he*
is played by the same actor

SHEIKH. Ah! A house of
heavenly peace! I rent it!

OMNES. You!

FLAVIA. Is it?

SHEIKH (*with dignity*): Is
me? Certainly is me! Who
else?

to tell you, because as
soon as that curtain's down
you'll be round seeing her,
I know that. Well, she's
being difficult, isn't she—
I saw you with that cactus
—I'm not blind. And then
you'll be on the next train
back to London. I'm
afraid I'm starting to know
the way you operate, you
see, Lloyd—and I bet
there's someone else, in
Richard III, isn't there, but
you can't just walk away
from it this time!

LLOYD *wearily, smilingly,
soothingly gestures that
he can't hear a word.*

POPPY (*out loud*): Well, I'm
sorry, but you've *got* to
hear, because I'm *pregnant!*

*A gasp from everyone on
stage. They both become
aware that the act has
ended.*

LLOYD (*whispers*): And
curtain!

POPPY *runs back to the
corner.*

LLOYD *subsides, defeated,
on to the cactus.*

Curtain.

BURGLAR. And what you're
up to with my little girl
down there in Basingstoke
I won't ask. But I'll tell
you one thing, Vicki.

VICKI. What's that, Dad?

BURGLAR. When all around
is strife and uncertainty,
there's nothing like . . .

He takes MRS CLACKETT'*s
plate.*

BURGLAR. . . . . a good old-
fashioned plate of sardines!

Curtain.

Act Three

ACT ONE

The living-room of the Brents' country home. Wednesday afternoon.
(Municipal Theatre, Stockton-on-Tees, Saturday April 6.)

This time the act is being seen from the front again, exactly as it was
the first time, at the rehearsal in Weston-super-Mare. Before the
curtain rises we hear the last of the front-of-house calls.

POPPY (*over the Tannoy*): Ladies and gentlemen, will you please take
your seats. The performance is about to . . . oh.

She stops because the curtain has risen to reveal TIM *checking the*
props on stage. The curtain hovers uncertainly, then descends.
When it rises again, the stage is empty and the telephone is
ringing.

Enter from the service quarters MRS CLACKETT, *pursued by*
BELINDA'*s foot. She is carrying an imposing plate of sardines, and*
she is limping painfully.

MRS CLACKETT. It's no good you going on. I can't pick sardines off
the floor *and* answer the phone. I've only got one leg. (*Into*
phone:) Hello . . . Yes, but there's no one here, love . . . No, Mr
Brent's not here . . . He lives here, yes, but he don't live here
now because he lives in Spain . . .

She tries to examine her knee as she talks.

Mr Philip Brent, that's right . . . The one that writes the plays,
only why he wants to get mixed up in plays God only knows, he'd

be safer off in the lion's cage at the zoo . . . No, she's in Spain, too, they're all in Spain, there's no one here . . . Am I in Spain? No, I'm not in Spain, dear, I'm in agony. That's where I am. One moment I'm standing there with a plate of sardines, next moment she's kicked me on the kneecap and there's sardines all over the floor.

The plate tips as she rubs her knee, and the sardines slide unnoticed on to the floor.

Here we are, we haven't been going three months, and already she's lashing out with her feet, and here am I, I don't know where I am, I'm eating sardines off the floor with one knee, don't tell us they've gone again . . .

She looks round for the sardines.

. . . and if you want anything else you'll have to ring the house-agents, because they've got their hands free to see what they're doing . . . No, they're not in Spain, they're next to the phone in the study. Squire, Squire, Hackham, and hold on, I'm going to do something wrong here, I can't think with one hand.

She shuffles phone, plate, and newspaper uncertainly.

Always the same, isn't it. You've got too much on your plate, and next thing you know you've put your foot in it.

She puts her foot in it.

Oh, speak of the devil. (*Wipes her shoe on the newspaper.*) They'll all want to go putting their foot in it now, won't they. (*Drops the newspaper over the sardines.*) I'll put that there, look. That'll keep them out of harm's way. But what I'm holding now I *don't* know . . .

Exit into the study, holding the empty plate and the telephone receiver. The body of the phone falls off its table and follows halfway to the door. The sound of a key in the lock. The front door opens. On the doorstep stands ROGER, *carrying a cardboard box.*

ROGER. . . . My housekeeper, yes, but this is her afternoon off.

The body of the phone begins to creep inconspicuously towards the door.

Enter VICKI.

So we've got the place entirely to ourselves.

ROGER *goes back and brings in a flight bag and closes the front door.*

I'll just check.

He halts the telephone with a casually placed foot. VICKI *gazes round.*

Hello? Anyone at home? No, there's no one here.

He picks the phone up, and puts it back on its table.

So what do you think?

He takes his hand off the phone, and it springs back on to the floor.

VICKI. Great. And this is all yours?

The phone starts to creep away again. ROGER *casually picks it up as he talks and puts it down on the sideboard.*

ROGER. Just a little shack in the woods, really. Converted posset mill. Sixteenth-century.

VICKI. It must have cost a bomb.

Another jerk on the wire catapults the phone across the room. VICKI *pays no attention to it.*

ROGER. Well, one has to have somewhere to entertain one's business associates. Someone on the phone now, by the look of it.

He picks the phone up and puts it back on the sideboard.

It's probably this, you know, this Arab saying he wants to come at four, so I mean I'll just have a word with him and . . .

He tries to pick up the receiver and finds that it's not there. As the conversation continues he follows the receiver cord along with his hand.

VICKI. Right, and I've got to get those files to our Basingstoke office by four.

ROGER. Yes, we'll only just manage to pick it in. I mean, we'll only just fit it up. I mean . . .

VICKI. Right, then.

ROGER. We won't bother to pull the champagne.

He pulls gently at the cord.

VICKI. All these doors.

ROGER. Oh, only a handful, really. Study. Kitchens, and a self-contained service flat for the . . .

He tugs hard, and the cord comes away without the receiver.

. . . receiver.

VICKI. Terrific. And which one's the . . . ?

ROGER. What?

VICKI. You know . . .

ROGER. Oh. Through here.

Opens the downstairs bathroom for her.

VICKI. Fantastic.

Exit VICKI *into the bathroom.* ROGER *tosses the phone casually off after her.*
Enter MRS CLACKETT *from the study, still walking with difficulty, and holding the now cordless receiver and a small shovel.*

MRS CLACKETT. I've just come for my sardines.

Mutual surprise. ROGER *closes the door to the bathroom, and tries to slip the champagne into the bag, but finds it's in there already.*

ROGER. I'm sorry. I thought there was no one here.

MRS CLACKETT. I'm not here. (*Looks round for the phone, so that she can replace the receiver.*) I don't know *where* I am.

ROGER. I'm from the agents.

MRS CLACKETT. Lost the phone now.

ROGER. Squire, Squire, Hackham, and Dudley.

MRS CLACKETT. Never lost a phone before.

ROGER. I'm Tramplemain.

MRS CLACKETT. I'll just put it up here, look, if anyone wants it.

She puts the receiver in some handy prominent place.

ROGER. Oh, right, thanks. No, I just dropped in to . . . go into a few things. Well, to check some of the measurements. Do one or two odd jobs.

The bathroom door opens. ROGER *closes it.* MRS CLACKETT *looks under the newspaper, then turns round to look for the plate.*

MRS CLACKETT. Now the plate's gone.

ROGER. Oh, and a client. I'm showing a prospective client over the house.

VICKI (*off, opening the door*): What's wrong with this door?

ROGER. She's thinking of renting it. Her interest is definitely aroused

Enter VICKI *from the bathroom.*
ROGER *steps on to the newspaper.*

VICKI. That's not the bedroom.

ROGER. The bedroom? No, that's the downstairs bathroom and WC suite. And this is the housekeeper. Mrs Crockett.

MRS CLACKETT. Sardines, dear, sardines.

VICKI. Oh. Hi.

ROGER. She's not really here.

MRS CLACKETT. Only you're standing on them.

ROGER (*moves*): It's the royal, you know.

MRS CLACKETT (*looks under the newspaper*): Oh, you shouldn't have stood on them.

ROGER (*to* MRS CLACKETT): Don't worry about us.

MRS CLACKETT. Only I need these sardines, you see.

ROGER. We'll just inspect the house.

MRS CLACKETT. I'll have to give the floor a wash now.

Exit MRS CLACKETT *into study leaving the sardines beneath the newspaper on the floor.*

ROGER. I'm sorry about this.

VICKI. That's all right. We don't want the television, do we?

ROGER. Television? That's right, television, she didn't explain about wanting to watch this royal, you know, because obviously there's been this thing with the . . . (*Indicates the sardines.*) I mean, I'm just, you know, in case anyone's looking at all this and thinking, 'My God!'.

VICKI. Great. Come on, then. (*Starts upstairs.*) I've got to be in Basingstoke by four.

ROGER. Sorry, love. I thought we ought to get that straight.

VICKI. We'll take it up with us.

ROGER. Where are we?

VICKI. And don't let my files out of sight.

ROGER. Hold on. We've got out of . . .

VICKI. What?

ROGER. What?

VICKI. Her?

ROGER. Her? OK—'her'. Right, because she has been in the family for generations.

Enter MRS CLACKETT *from the study, carrying a bottle of whisky.*

MRS CLACKETT. Sardines . . . sardines . . . I'll just give the floor a wash with this, look, and they'll be out of your way. (*Finds the bottle in her hands.*) Look what I've got hold of now!

VICKI. Oh. Great.

MRS CLACKETT. It's like a battlefield out there.

VICKI. Terrific.

MRS CLACKETT *puts the bottle of whisky with the other bottles on the sideboard.*

MRS CLACKETT. I'll put it here, look, then if he wants it he won't know where to find it. Sardines, sardines. You'll have to do the sardines, then, 'cause I've got to go back to the kitchen now and do some more sardines.

Exit MRS CLACKETT *to service quarters.*

VICKI. You see? She thinks it's great. She's even making us sardines!

ROGER. OK, so what do you think?

VICKI. I think she's terrific.

ROGER. No, I mean, do you want to do the . . . ? (*Indicates the sardines.*)

VICKI. So which way?

ROGER. I don't know. Kind of parcel them up in the, you know.

VICKI. Up here?

ROGER. I mean, I've got to do the . . . (*Indicates the bag and box.*)

VICKI. In here?

ROGER. OK, you take the . . . (*Bag and box.*) I'll do the . . . (*Sardines.*)

Exit VICKI *into mezzanine bathroom, still unable to deviate by a hair's breadth from the script.* ROGER *parcels up the sardines in the newspaper as best he can.*

VICKI. It's another bathroom.

She reappears.

ROGER. Box! Bag!

VICKI. Always trying to get me into bathrooms.

ROGER. Bag! Box!

Exit VICKI *into linen cupboard.*
ROGER *runs upstairs with the parcel of sardines.*
Enter VICKI *from linen cupboard.*

VICKI. This is the airing cupboard.

ROGER. Box! Box! Bag! Bag!

VICKI. Oh, you're in a real state!

ROGER. If we haven't got the, you know, upstairs, I mean, my God!

> ROGER *runs downstairs, puts the parcel of sardines on the telephone table, and picks up the bag and box.*

VICKI. You can't even get the door open.

> *Exit* VICKI *into bedroom.*
> *The sound of a key in the lock. The door opens, and on the doorstep stands* PHILIP, *carrying a cardboard box.*

PHILIP. Yes, but this is Mrs Clackett's afternoon off.

> ROGER *abandons the sardines and flees upstairs with the bag and the box. He finds the bedroom door shut in his face.*
> *Enter* FLAVIA.

We've got the place entirely to ourselves.

> *Exit* ROGER *into the bedroom with the bag and box.*
> PHILIP *brings in the flight bag.*

FLAVIA. Look at it!

PHILIP. Do you like it?

FLAVIA. I can't believe it!

PHILIP. The perfect place for an assignation.

FLAVIA. Home.

PHILIP. Home.

FLAVIA (*produces the remains of the phone*): But how odd to find the telephone in the garden!

PHILIP. I'll put it back.

> *She hands him the phone—now in a very deteriorated condition— and he attempts to replace it on the telephone table. But it is still connected to its lead, which is too short, since it runs out through the downstairs bathroom door, and back in through the front door.*

FLAVIA. I thought I'd better bring it in.

PHILIP. Very sensible.

He tugs discreetly at the lead.

FLAVIA. Someone's bound to want it.

PHILIP. Oh dear. (*Tugs.*)

FLAVIA. Why don't you put it back on the table?

PHILIP. The wire seems to be caught.

FLAVIA. Oh, look, it's caught round the downstairs bathroom.

PHILIP. So it is.

> FLAVIA *turns and with discreet violence pulls the lead out of the junction-box where it originates.* PHILIP, *meanwhile, takes the phone back out of the front door, and re-emerges with it through the downstairs bathroom.*

FLAVIA. I think I've disentangled it.

PHILIP. I climbed through the bathroom window and . . . oh . . . oh . . .

> *He takes the parcel of sardines off the telephone table and puts the telephone in its place.*

FLAVIA. Anyway, our little secret hideaway.

PHILIP. The last place on earth anyone will . . .

> *Attempting to fold up the newspaper briskly and tidily, he becomes distracted by the contents that come oozing out over his hands.*

FLAVIA. . . . look for us, yes, but it's rather funny, creeping in like this.

> *Pause.*

PHILIP. Sorry?

FLAVIA. I know what you're thinking. You're thinking, 'It's damned serious!'

PHILIP. Sorry. Yes. It's damned serious!

FLAVIA. You're thinking about Inland Revenue.

PHILIP. Absolutely. Inland Revenue. Well, to cut a long story short, I think I'm going to have a wash and go to bed.

He puts down the parcel of sardines on the sofa, picks up the bag and box, and starts upstairs.

FLAVIA (*hurriedly*): Yes, but Inland Revenue! We must have our little talk first about Inland Revenue! Because you're thinking something like, 'If Inland Revenue finds out we're in the country, even for one night, bang goes our claim to be resident abroad, bang goes most of this year's . . . Leave those!

PHILIP drops the bag and box, but by this time he is already upstairs.

Downstairs!

PHILIP. Sh!

FLAVIA. Not upstairs!

PHILIP. Inland Revenue may hear us! What?

Enter MRS CLACKETT from the service quarters carrying a fresh plate of sardines.

MRS CLACKETT (*to herself*): One moment they're kicking you to death, next moment they expect you to come waltzing in with more sardines.

She puts down the plate of sardines, and goes to sit on the sofa, on the parcel of sardines left there by PHILIP.

PHILIP (*urgently, looking down from the gallery*): Mrs Newspaper!

MRS CLACKETT jumps up just in time.

MRS CLACKETT. Oh, you give me a turn! My heart jumped right out of the sofa!

PHILIP. So did mine!

FLAVIA. We thought you'd gone!

MRS CLACKETT (*finds the parcel of sardines and examines it*): I thought you was in Sardinia!

PHILIP. We are! We are!

FLAVIA. You haven't seen us!

PHILIP. We're not here!

MRS CLACKETT. Oh, look, and they've brought me a present home!

FLAVIA. Yes, but the main thing is that the income tax people are after us.

MRS CLACKETT. I can guess which one of them thought of this.

FLAVIA. We're not here. You haven't seen us.

MRS CLACKETT. Lovely helping of mashed sardines.

FLAVIA. Anyway, if anybody asks for us, you don't know nothing. Anything.

MRS CLACKETT. She just leaves them quietly on the sofa.

FLAVIA. So we're off to bed.

MRS CLACKETT. And goes off without waiting to be thanked.

FLAVIA. Has the bed been aired?

MRS CLACKETT. Well, I've got a little surprise for *you*, love. (*Pursues her upstairs.*)

FLAVIA. No? I'll get a hot water bottle.

Exit FLAVIA *into the mezzanine bathroom.*

MRS CLACKETT. I'll give you sardines, my sweetheart.

MRS CLACKETT *runs back downstairs and exits into the study with the parcel of sardines.*

PHILIP. Oh . . .

Enter FLAVIA *hurriedly from the mezzanine bathroom.*

FLAVIA. So now she's left you all on your own, has she?

PHILIP. Well . . .

FLAVIA. What are you supposed to do? Talk to yourself?

PHILIP. Oh dear.

FLAVIA. Has she told you what she's done with your letters?

Enter MRS CLACKETT *from the study, still holding the parcel of sardines.*

MRS CLACKETT. What's she telling you now, love?

FLAVIA (*to* MRS CLACKETT): You haven't told him about his letters! (*To* PHILIP:) She's put them all in the study! All the letters from the income tax!

PHILIP. Oh dear.

MRS CLACKETT. Telling him where his letters are! You don't own him, you know!

She advances on FLAVIA *with the parcel of sardines.*

FLAVIA (*retreating*): She's put them all in the little pigeonhouse!

Exit FLAVIA *into the mezzanine bathroom.*

PHILIP. In the pigeonhouse?

MRS CLACKETT. Pigeonhole, dear. You come with me. Anybody would think she was married to you.

MRS CLACKETT leads PHILIP firmly off into the study, still carrying the parcel of sardines. PHILIP's bag and box are left outside the bedroom door.
Enter ROGER from the bedroom, still dressed, but with no tie on.

ROGER. Yes, but I could hear voices!

He falls over PHILIP's bag and box.
Enter VICKI from the bedroom in her underwear.

VICKI. Voices? What sort of voices?

ROGER. Box voices. I mean, *people's* boxes.

VICKI. But there's no one here.

ROGER. Darling, I saw the door-handle move! And these bags—I'm not sure they were, you know, when we went into the, do you know what I mean?

VICKI. I still don't see why you've got to put your tie on to look.

ROGER (*picks up the bag and box*): Because if someone left these things outside the, I mean, come *on*, they obviously want them downstairs inside the, you know.

VICKI. Mrs Clockett?

ROGER. It could be. Coming up here on her way to, well, carrying various, I mean, who knows?

VICKI (*looks over the bannisters*): Oh look, she's opened our sardines.

She moves to go downstairs. ROGER *puts down the bag and box outside the linen cupboard door and grabs her.*

ROGER. Come back!

VICKI. What?

ROGER. I'll fetch them! You can't go downstairs like that.

VICKI. Why not?

ROGER. Mrs Crackett.

VICKI. Mrs Crackett?

ROGER. She's irreplaceable.

Enter MRS CLACKETT *from the study, without the parcel of sardines, wiping her hands.*

MRS CLACKETT (*to herself*): At least I've thanked her properly for the sardines.

ROGER *tries to pull open the linen cupboard door to conceal* VICKI, *but it is obstructed by the bag and box.*

Oh, you're still poking around, are you?

ROGER. Yes, still poking, well, still pulling.

He tugs at the door again, unaware of the obstruction, and the handle comes off.

MRS CLACKETT. Good job I can't see far with this leg.

ROGER *moves the bag and box, gets the door of the linen cupboard open one way or another and* VICKI *inside, and rebalances the handle in place.*

ROGER. Just, you know, trying all the doors and I mean checking all the door-handles.

He starts downstairs, carrying PHILIP's *bag and box.*

Mrs Blackett . . .

MRS CLACKETT. Clackett, dear, Clackett.

ROGER. Mrs Clackett. Is there anyone else in the house, Mrs Clackett?

MRS CLACKETT. I haven't seen no one, dear.

ROGER. I thought I heard a box. I mean, I found these voices.

MRS CLACKETT. Voices? There's no voices here, love.

ROGER. I must have imagined it.

PHILIP (off): Oh my God!

The sound of a body falling, off, followed by a wailing groan from PHILIP.

ROGER. I beg your pardon?

MRS CLACKETT (*mimics* PHILIP): Oh my God! (*She crashes things about on the sideboard in imitation of the offstage crash, and ends the performance with a wailing groan.*)

ROGER. Why, what is it?

MRS CLACKETT. The study door's open.

She crosses and closes it.

ROGER. They're going to want these inside the . . . (*Indicates the study.*) So I'll put them outside the . . . (*Indicates the front door.*) Then they can, do you know what I mean?

Exit ROGER *through the front door, carrying the bag and box.*
Enter FLAVIA *from the mezzanine bathroom, carrying a first-aid box. She sees the linen cupboard door swinging open as she passes, and pushes it shut, so that the latch closes. The handle comes off in her hand.*

FLAVIA. Nothing but flapping doors in this handle.

Exit FLAVIA *into the bedroom, holding the first-aid box and the handle.*
Enter from the study PHILIP, *holding a tax demand and its envelope. The part is now being played not by* FREDERICK *but by* TIM.

PHILIP. '. . . final notice . . . steps will be taken . . . distraint . . .
proceedings in court . . .'

MRS CLACKETT. Oh my Lord, who are you?

PHILIP. I'm Philip.

MRS CLACKETT. You're Philip? What's happened to *you?*

PHILIP. Well, there were these sardines on the floor . . .

MRS CLACKETT. And he stepped in it!

PHILIP. And I slipped . . .

MRS CLACKETT. She's killed him! She's killed you!

PHILIP. No. He's just a bit shaken. I'll be all right in a minute.

Exit MRS CLACKETT *into the study.*

MRS CLACKETT (*off*). What? Philip. You weren't going to tell me a
gentleman had come about the house, were you?

Enter MRS CLACKETT

MRS CLACKETT. That's right. A gentleman come about the house.

PHILIP. Don't tell me. I'm not here.

MRS CLACKETT. You haven't done himself an injury, then?

PHILIP. Leave everything to Squire, Squire, Hackham, and Dudley.

MRS CLACKETT. All right, love. Oh, and he's put your box out in the
garden for you.

PHILIP. Let them do anything. Just so long as you don't tell anyone
we're here.

MRS CLACKETT. So I'll just sit down and turn on the . . . sardines,
I've forgotten the sardines! (*Finds the sardines on the table, where
they should be.*) Oh, no, I haven't, I've remembered the sardines!
What a surprise! I must go out to the kitchen and make another
plate of sardines to celebrate.

Exit MRS CLACKETT *to the service quarters.*

PHILIP. I didn't get this! I'm not here. I'm in Spain. But if I didn't
get it I didn't open it.

Enter FLAVIA *from the bedroom. She is holding the dress that* VICKI *arrived in, and the handle of the linen cupboard.*

FLAVIA. Darling . . . (*She stares at* TIM *in surprise, then recovers herself and looks at the dress.*) I never had a handle like this, did I?

PHILIP (*abstracted*): Didn't you?

FLAVIA. I shouldn't buy anything as tarty as this . . .

FLAVIA *drops the dress and attempts to replace the handle on the linen cupboard behind her back.*

Oh, it's not something you gave me, is it?

PHILIP. I should never have touched it.

FLAVIA. No, it's lovely.

PHILIP. Stick it down. Put it back. Never saw it.

Exit PHILIP *into study.*

FLAVIA. Well, I'll put it in the attic, if anyone else wants to have a try.

Exit FLAVIA *along the upstairs corridor, taking the handle but leaving the dress on the floor.*
Enter ROGER *through the front door, without the bag and box.*

ROGER. All right, all right . . . Now the study door's open again! What's going on?

He goes towards the study, but stops at the sound of urgent knocking overhead.

Knocking! (*Knocking*) Upstairs!

Runs upstairs. Knocking.

Oh my God, there's something in the . . . (*Discovers the lack of a handle.*) Oh my God! (*Knocking*) Listen! I can't, because the handle seems to have, you know. You'll just have to . . .

He demonstrates pushing. Knocking.

Come on! Come on!

Knocking.

I mean, whatever it is in there. Can you hear me? Darling!

Knocking.

Look, don't just keep banging! There's nothing I can, I mean it won't, there's nowhere to . . .

Knocking.

Listen! Climb round into the . . . (*Indicates the bedroom.*) Squeeze through the, you know, and shin down the, I mean, there must be some way!

Knocking.

ROGER. Oh, for God's sake!

Exit ROGER *into the bedroom.*
Enter PHILIP *from the study, holding a tax demand and an envelope. He is now being played by* FREDERICK, *with a plaster on his forehead and another bloodstained plaster over his nose.*

PHILIP. '. . . final notice . . . steps will be taken . . . distraint . . . proceedings in court . . .'

Enter ROGER *from the bedroom, pulling* VICKI *after him.* PHILIP *gazes at them, baffled.*

ROGER. Oh, it's you.

VICKI. Of course it's me! You put me in here! In the dark, with all black sheets and things.

ROGER. I put you in *there*, but you managed to squeeze through the, you know.

VICKI. Why did *I* lock the door? Why did *you* lock the door!

ROGER. I couldn't, I mean, look, look, it's come off!

VICKI. *Someone* locked the door!

PHILIP. Sorry.

Exit PHILIP *apologetically into study.*

ROGER. Anyway, we can't stand here like this.

VICKI. Like what?

ROGER. I mean, you know, with people going in and out.

VICKI. OK, I'll take it off.

ROGER. In here, in here!

Ushers her into the bedroom.
Enter PHILIP cautiously from the study, holding the tax demand and the envelope.

PHILIP. '. . . final notice . . . steps will be taken . . . distraint . . . proceedings in court . . .'

Enter ROGER from the bedroom, holding the first aid box.
He looks up and down the landing.
Enter VICKI from the bedroom.
PHILIP stares at them.

VICKI. Now what?

ROGER. A hot water box! *I* didn't put it there!

VICKI. *I* didn't put it there.

PHILIP. Sorry.

Exit PHILIP into the study.

ROGER. Someone in the bathroom, filling first aid bottles.

Exit ROGER into the mezzanine bathroom.

VICKI (*anxious*): You don't think there's something creepy going on?

Exit VICKI into mezzanine bathroom.
Enter FLAVIA along the upstairs corridor.

FLAVIA. Darling . . . Darling?

Enter PHILIP cautiously from the study. He raises the income tax demand to speak.

Darling, are you coming to bed or aren't you?

Exit FLAVIA into bedroom.
Enter ROGER and VICKI from the mezzanine bathroom.
PHILIP raises his income tax demand to speak.

ROGER. What did you say?

VICKI. I didn't say anything.

Exit PHILIP *into the study.*

ROGER. I mean, there's the door handle. Now there's the first water box.

VICKI. I can feel goose-pimples all over.

ROGER. Yes, quick, get something round you.

VICKI. Get the covers over our heads.

ROGER *is about to open the bedroom door.*

ROGER. Just a moment. What did I do with those sardines?

He goes downstairs. VICKI *makes to follow.*

You—wait here.

VICKI (*uneasy*): You hear all sorts of funny things about these old houses.

ROGER. Yes, but this one has been extensively modernised throughout. I can't see how anything creepy would survive oil-fired central heating and . . .

VICKI. What? What is it?

ROGER *stares round in silence.*

What's happening?

ROGER. The sardines. They've gone. (*Sees them.*) No, they haven't. They're here. Oh. Well. My God—I mean—my God!

He turns and starts back upstairs. FLAVIA *crawls through the front door. She picks up the sardines and takes them back to the front door.*

You put a plate of sardines down for two minutes, and the last thing you expect to find, I mean, these days, the one thing you don't expect to find when you come back is a plate of, I mean that's *really* weird!

VICKI. Perhaps there is something funny going on. I'm going to get into bed and put my head under the . . .

She freezes at the sight of the empty table outside the bedroom door.

ROGER. Because, I mean, there they are! Exactly where I . . .

He realises that the sardines are not there.

VICKI. Bag . . .

ROGER goes back downstairs to investigate. VICKI runs after him. FLAVIA reacts to the mention of the bag.

ROGER. I suppose Mrs Sprockett must have, I mean, Jesus, what *is* going on?

As ROGER turns away towards VICKI, FLAVIA crawls hurriedly back in, puts the sardines on the table, and flees through the front door.

VICKI. Bag!

ROGER. Bag?

VICKI. Bag! Bag!

She drags ROGER back upstairs.

ROGER. What do you mean, bag, bag?

VICKI. Bag! Bag! Bag!

ROGER looks over the bannisters and sees the sardines.

ROGER. Sardines!

VICKI. Bag! Bag! Bag!

ROGER. Sardines! Sardines!

VICKI. Bag! Bag! Bag!

While ROGER is gazing at the sardines, and VICKI is looking at ROGER, the bedroom door opens, and FLAVIA puts the flight bag on the table outside.

ROGER (*tearing himself away from the sight of the sardines*): Bag? What bag?

VICKI (*gazing at the bag*): No bag!

ROGER. No bag?

VICKI. Your bag! Suddenly! Here! Now—gone!

ROGER. It's in the bedroom. (*Sees the bag.*) It *was* in the bedroom. I put it in the bedroom. I'll put it back in the bedroom.

As ROGER *goes to open the bedroom door it opens in front of him, and* FLAVIA *begins to come out carrying the box.*

VICKI. Don't go in there!

ROGER *grabs the box and closes the door.*

ROGER. The box!

VICKI. The box?

ROGER. They've *both* not gone!

VICKI. Oh! My files!

ROGER. What on earth is happening? Where's Mrs Spratchett?

He starts downstairs with the bag and box. VICKI *follows him.*

You wait in the bedroom.

VICKI. No! No! No!

She runs downstairs.

ROGER. Well, get dressed, then!

VICKI. I'm not going in there!

ROGER. I'll fetch your dress out here.

He puts the bag and box down at the head of stairs, returns to the bedroom, and sees the dress on the floor.
Exit ROGER *into the bedroom.*
Enter ROGER *from the bedroom.*

Your dress has gone.

As he speaks he slides the dress over the edge of the gallery with his foot to get rid of it. It falls on top of VICKI *beneath.*

VICKI (*struggling beneath it*): Oh!

ROGER. Don't panic! Don't panic! There's some perfectly rational explanation for all this . . .

He starts downstairs, looking over the bannister appalled at the sight of VICKI *below, and falls headlong over the bag and box at the top of the stairs.*
Exit VICKI *blindly through the front door with the dress.*
Enter PHILIP *from the study, still played by* FREDERICK.
He is holding a tax demand in his right hand, and one of the plates of sardines in his left.

PHILIP. Darling, I know this is going to sound silly, but . . .

His struggles to get the tax demand unstuck from his fingers, die away at the sight of ROGER, *lying at the bottom of the stairs.*
Enter FLAVIA *along the upstairs corridor, carrying further pieces of bric-a-brac.*

FLAVIA. Darling, if we're not going to bed I'm going to clear out the attic . . .

PHILIP (*to* ROGER): Are you all right?

FLAVIA. Oh my God!

She rushes downstairs.

PHILIP. What happened?

FLAVIA. Can you speak, love?

Enter MRS CLACKETT *in alarm from the service quarters, holding another plate of sardines.*

MRS CLACKETT. Oh, she's killed this one now!

FLAVIA. He's stunned, that's all. Keep going.

ROGER (*lifts his head*): Don't panic! Don't panic!

FLAVIA. He's all right!

PHILIP. Well done.

MRS CLACKETT. She'll get you next time.

FLAVIA. Just keep going.

ROGER. There's some perfectly rational explanation for all this.

PHILIP. Where are we?

ROGER. I'll fetch Mrs Splotchett and she'll tell us what's happening . . .

MRS CLACKETT. You've fetched her. I'm here.

ROGER. I've fetched Mrs Splotchett and she'll tell us what's happening.

MRS CLACKETT. She won't, you know.

PHILIP. Oh dear.

FLAVIA. *I'll* tell you what's happening.

ROGER. There's a man in there! Yes?

FLAVIA. He's not in there, my precious—he's in here, look, and so am I.

MRS CLACKETT. No, no, there's no one in the house, love. Yes?

FLAVIA. No, look, I know this is a great surprise for everyone. I mean, it's quite a shock for *us*, finding a man lying at the bottom of the stairs! (*To* PHILIP:) Isn't it, darling?

PHILIP. Oh dear.

FLAVIA. But now we've all met we'll just have to—well, we'll just have to introduce ourselves! Won't we, darling?

PHILIP. Oh dear. Oh dear.

FLAVIA. This is my husband. I'm afraid he hates surprises! So, darling, why don't you go off and get the bottle marked poison in the downstairs loo? That eats through anything.

PHILIP. Eats through anything. Right. Thank you. Thank you. Yes, I've heard of people getting stuck with a problem, but this is ridiculous.

He opens the downstairs bathroom door to go off.
A pane of glass drops neatly out of the mullioned window, and an arm comes through and releases the catch. The window opens, and through it appears the BURGLAR, *played by* TIM.

BURGLAR. No bars. No burglar alarms. They ought to be prosecuted for incitement.

He climbs in, and looks round in surprise to find the room full of people.

MRS CLACKETT. Come in and join the party, love.

FLAVIA. A burglar! This is most exciting!

PHILIP. This is my fault. Because when I say, 'I've heard of people getting stuck with a problem, but this is ridiculous,' and I open this door . . .

He opens the downstairs bathroom again. A pane of glass drops neatly out of the mullioned window, and an arm comes through. Enter through the window the BURGLAR, played by SELSDON.

BURGLAR SELSDON. No bars. No burglar alarms. They ought to be prosecuted for incitement.

He climbs in, becoming uneasily aware of the others as he does so.

PHILIP. Oh dear, I've done it again.

BURGLAR SELSDON. No, but sometimes it makes me want to sit down and weep.

MRS CLACKETT. I know, love, it's getting like a funeral in here.

BURGLAR SELSDON. When I think I used to do banks!

FLAVIA. Just keep going.

BURGLAR SELSDON *and* BURGLAR TIM (*together*): When I remember I used to bullion vaults!

PHILIP. Oh dear oh dear oh dear.

THE TWO BURGLARS (*together*): What am I doing now?—I'm breaking into paper bags . . .

FLAVIA. Keep going.

BURGLAR SELSDON. Stop?

FLAVIA. No, no!

BURGLAR SELSDON. I thought the coast was clear, you see. I saw him going out to the bathroom.

FLAVIA (*closes the downstairs bathroom door*): It's all right. We'll think of something.

BURGLAR SELSDON. Oh, no, I was listening most carefully. What's it he says?

PHILIP. 'I've heard of people getting stuck with a problem, but this is ridiculous.'

BURGLAR SELSDON. And he opened the door . . .

> BURGLAR SELSDON *opens the downstairs bathroom door to demonstrate.*
> *A pane of glass drops out of the mullioned window, and an arm comes through.*
> *Enter through the window the* BURGLAR, *played by* LLOYD.

BURGLAR LLOYD. No bars. No burglar alarms. They ought to be prosecuted for incitement.

> *He climbs in, very uncertain what's happening to him. He doesn't know whether to react to the presence of the others or not.*

PHILIP. Oh no!

MRS CLACKETT. They always come in threes, don't they.

ALL THREE BURGLARS. When I think I used to do banks! When I remember I used to do bullion vaults . . .

FLAVIA. Hold on! We know this man! He's not a burglar! He's our social worker!

ROGER. He's *what?*

FLAVIA. He's that nice man who comes in and tells us what to do!

LLOYD. I've been working on Richard III for the last six weeks . . .

MRS CLACKETT. You think he needs working on more than we do?

BURGLAR SELSDON. *He's* the burglar now, is he?

MRS CLACKETT. No, no.

BURGLAR SELSDON. Got the sack, have I?

FLAVIA. No, no, no!

LLOYD. OK. OK. I'll think of something. (*Takes out his pills. To* MRS CLACKETT:) Fetch the sardines!

MRS CLACKETT. I've fetched the sardines!

LLOYD. You've fetched the sardines?

OMNES. She's fetched the sardines!

PHILIP. Oh dear.

LLOYD (*to* PHILIP): Get the tax demand!

OMNES. He's got the tax demand!

LLOYD. Right, then, I suggest . . . (*Takes a pill.*) I suggest . . .

> FLAVIA *hands him a glass of whisky to wash the pill down. He gulps at the whisky without thinking.*

I suggest . . .

> *He becomes unable to speak or breathe, and only now realises that it's whisky he has swallowed.*

BURGLAR SELSDON. We're doing it, are we?

FLAVIA. What?

BURGLAR SELSDON. Richard III?

> LLOYD *tries to speak.*

MRS CLACKETT. What's he saying?

FLAVIA. He's saying . . . ring the police!

ROGER. Ring the police?

OMNES. Ring the police!

> ROGER *picks up the receiver, finds the body of the phone is missing, and hands the receiver on to* LLOYD.

ROGER. It's for you.

> LLOYD *puts the receiver to his ear and tries to dial.*

FLAVIA. No phone?

MRS CLACKETT (*to* TIM): Fetch a phone!

TIM. Fetch a phone?

> *Exit* TIM *through the front door.*

FLAVIA. Here's the phone!

ROGER (*hands* LLOYD *the phone*): We've found the phone!

LLOYD *puts the receiver back on top of the phone. At once it rings.*

FLAVIA. Pick it up!

LLOYD (*faintly*): Pick it up?

OMNES. Pick it up!

FLAVIA (*picks it up*): It's the police! I'll tell them we're just missing a young woman!

ROGER. Yes! We're just missing a young woman!

Enter VICKI *through the window.*

VICKI. It's in the garden now, and it's a man!

MRS CLACKETT. Oh, it's her! We'd forgotten all about her!

VICKI. No, he almost saw me!

FLAVIA (*to* VICKI): All right. (*To* LLOYD:) So what do you say to that, my sweet?

LLOYD (*faintly*): I've got to get the 8.40 back to London.

LLOYD *opens the door to flee, but recoils, because there on the doorstep stands the* SHEIKH, *played by* POPPY.

MRS CLACKETT. Oh, it's the other one! And in her wedding dress!

OMNES. Oh!

FLAVIA. Yes! Yes! It's their wedding day! What a happy ending!

OMNES. Ah!

LLOYD *and* POPPY *are hurriedly ushered down centre.*

FLAVIA. They just want to be alone in their new home. If only someone would . . .

She opens the downstairs bathroom door to demonstrate the action to the wings.

. . . pull the shades!

Enter TIM *from the open downstairs bathroom, dressed in the black sheets.*

TIM (*uncertainly*): Come on?

MRS CLACKETT. Oh, and here's the mother of the bride!

TIM. Go off?

OMNES (*demonstrating*): Pull the shades!

Exit TIM *into the wings.*

BURGLAR SELSDON. Last line?

OMNES. Last line!

BURGLAR SELSDON (*crosses to* VICKI): But I'll tell you one thing, Vicki.

Slaps her on the back, and she loses her lenses.

OMNES. What's that, Dad?

BURGLAR SELSDON. When all around is strife and uncertainty, there's nothing like . . . (*Takes the sardines.*) . . . a good old-fashioned plate of curtain!

Down comes the curtain—and jams just above the level of their heads. As one man they seize hold of it and drag it down to the ground.

Curtain.